Twayne's United States Authors Series

EDITOR OF THIS VOLUME

Kenneth E. Eble

University of Utah

Daniel Fuchs

TUSAS 333

Daniel Fuchs

DANIEL FUCHS

By GABRIEL MILLER

Illinois State University

TWAYNE PUBLISHERS
A DIVISION OF G. K. HALL & CO., BOSTON

Copyright © 1979 by G. K. Hall & Co.

Published in 1979 by Twayne Publishers,
A Division of G. K. Hall & Co.
All Rights Reserved

Printed on permanent/durable acid-free paper and bound
in the United States of America

First Printing

Frontispiece photograph of Daniel Fuchs by Julien Wasser

Library of Congress Cataloging in Publication Data

Miller, Gabriel, 1948-
Daniel Fuchs.

(Twayne's United States authors series ;TUSAS 333)
Bibliography: p. 164-68
Includes index.
1. Fuchs, Daniel, 1909-   —Criticism and interpretation.
PS3511.U27Z77   813'.52   78-32106
ISBN 0-8057-7240-5

This book is for my mother and father and in memory of Frieda Pauker and Sydney Miller, who have already spent their "summer in Williamsburg."

Contents

About the Author

Gabriel Miller was born in the Bronx, grew up and went to school there, and received a B.A. in English from Queens College of the City University of New York. He received his Ph.D. from Brown University (1975), where he also taught as a graduate assistant. He has taught literature and film at Arizona State University, and currently teaches at Illinois State University.

He has published articles on Alfred Hitchcock, Woody Allen, Albert Maltz, and Alvah Bessie. His book, *American Fiction Rediscovered in Film,* will be published by Frederick Ungar Publishing Company. At present he is working on a study of the literary careers of Alvah Bessie, Samuel Ornitz, Albert Maltz, and Dalton Trumbo, entitled *Four of the Ten.*

Preface

This is the first full-length study of an important writer who has been unjustly ignored by critics and scholars for decades. Rarely is Daniel Fuchs mentioned in studies of American fiction, and if mentioned, he is merely named or listed, never discussed. Studies dealing with the literature of the 1930s and even studies of American-Jewish fiction ignore him or only mention him in passing, when he should be singled out among the best artists in either classification. This study is designed to begin to rectify this error of neglect, to alert a wider audience to the richness and complexity of Fuchs's work.

Because this is the only study of the subject (except for Irving Howe's brief articles on Fuchs's novels), I have devoted most of my time to a thorough explication of the works, especially the novels *Summer in Williamsburg, Homage to Blenholt,* and *Low Company,* which represent Fuchs's greatest achievement as a writer. His fourth novel, *West of the Rockies,* and the short stories and essays are also discussed, but I have not dealt with his screen work, which should be the subject of another study. Nor have I dwelt much on the social backgrounds of his fiction, for there are many books on the 1930s. Fuchs's work is what is most important here, and so the books themselves have remained the focus of my attention.

In order to supply both an introduction to Fuchs's work and a critical treatment of it, I have chosen to proceed by a close reading of the texts, examining themes and literary connections and carefully following the development of Fuchs's world view. Simple chronological arrangement seemed best for this purpose, except that I found it necessary to group together his stories, some of which were published before the major fiction. Otherwise, I have given one chapter to each of the Williamsburg novels and one to the Hollywood writings, including *West of the Rockies.* The first chapter presents introductory information about Fuchs's life and about the artistic climate of the 1930s, the Yiddish influence on Fuchs's writing, and the relation of his work to that of Nathanael West.

There are a number of people I would like to thank for their help and encouragement. First is Professor David H. Hirsch of Brown University, who encouraged me to study the literature of the 1930s and to concentrate on Fuchs in particular, despite the feeling of many that Fuchs's work was not worthy of detailed study. Professors Barton St. Armand and George Monteiro were also very helpful with their suggestions and ideas. Special thanks to Professor Elmer Blistein, who was always willing to talk to me about the 1930s and its writers. Not least, this study owes a great deal to Daniel Fuchs himself, who patiently answered too many questions and subjected himself to an interview, and to his wife, Susan, who was a very gracious hostess to my wife and me during a visit to Los Angeles.

I must also single out for thanks the boys and girls in the back room who made the writing of this a real pleasure, filled with the best of memories: Tony and Elaine, David, Brenda, Tom and Jan, Mark, Bill, Tina, and Casey. Thanks, too, to Mary Ellen Chase for typing the manuscript.

My greatest debt is to my wife, my love, Kathy, who wrote more of this book than she would probably care to admit.

Chronology

1909   June 25, born in New York City, the fourth child of Jacob and Sara Fuchs.
1914   Family moves to Williamsburg.
1926   Family moves to Bensonhurst. Fuchs enters City College.
1930   Graduates from City College. "My Father's Story" published in *Brooklyn Daily Eagle*.
1931   "Where Al Capone Grew Up."
1932   Marries Susan Chessen.
1934   *Summer in Williamsburg*.
1936   *Homage to Blenholt*.
1937   *Low Company*. First trip to Hollywood.
1939   Son Jacob born.
1940   Goes to Hollywood to work on the screenplay of his story "The Fabulous Rubio."
1942   *The Big Shot* (his first screenplay credit).
1943   Enters military service; son Tom born.
1945   Discharged from the navy.
1947   *The Gangster*, based on his novel *Low Company*, appears as a film.
1955   Wins Academy Award for his screenplay of *Love Me or Leave Me*.
1956   *Stories* with Jean Stafford, William Maxwell, and John Cheever.
1958   First trip to London to work on films.
1961   Basic Books reissues the novels as *3 Novels by Daniel Fuchs*.
1962   Second trip to England to work on films.
1971   *West of the Rockies*.
1975   "Ivanov's 'The Adventures of a Fakir.'"
1979   *The Apathetic Bookie Joint*, a collection of stories including a previously unpublished novella *Triplicate* published by Methuen in September.

CHAPTER 1

"A Butterfly in the Subway"

DANIEL Fuchs was born in New York City on June 25, 1909. Life began on Rivington Street on Manhattan's Lower East Side,[1] a place inhabited primarily by immigrant Jews who had come there in flight from political persecution, pogroms, sorrow, hardship, and in search of the new prosperity that America seemed to promise.

The Lower East Side began to establish itself as a refuge for the East European Jewish community as early as the 1870s. It was a community bustling with activity, noisy and crowded. On Orchard Street and extending southward for blocks were numerous open-air markets selling "mostly articles of clothing at bargains frequently arrived at by heated, on the spot discussions."[2] There were pushcarts and peddlers, synagogues and sweatshops; the area was also the city's red-light district. In Michael Gold's words, it was "a tenement canyon, hung with fire escapes, bed clothing and faces."[3] The people who stayed there never made it in America: it was the home of the "Jews without money." It was also, however, the breeding ground of the labor movement and the center of many labor activities, producing such leaders and intellectuals as Michael Gold, Abraham Cahan, and Samuel Gompers.

Like most of the inhabitants of this section of New York City, Fuchs's parents were immigrants. His father, Jacob Fuchs, came to America from Russia when he was seventeen. At the time of Daniel's birth (he was the fifth child), he was recovering from the furriers' disease, and searching for a new way of making a living to support a large and growing family. He would soon become father to a set of twins.[4]

Fuchs's mother, Sarah Malkah, also immigrated in her teens (she was thirteen), from Poland. Like many immigrant children, she could come to America only when her father, who had preceded her, had earned enough money for her passage. In Holland, on her journey to America, she had been frightened by some soldiers, and the experi-

13

ence of traveling in steerage instilled in her a fear of the outside
world. Like many immigrant women she rarely ventured beyond her
own immediate neighborhood.[5]

There were four sons before Daniel: Rupert, Henry, Julie, and
George. Five days after Daniel was born, George fell off a roof and
was killed, and the Fuchs family, leaving behind that memory,
moved to New Lots. Daniel Fuchs recalls New Lots as an "empty
place with no houses, just large empty lots. There were many holes
and during rainy weather these holes would fill with water and
children would drown."[6]

The family did not stay in New Lots for very long. Across a bridge
that connected the Lower East Side with Brooklyn was Williamsburg, a new promised land which attracted many of the city's
poorer Jews, including the Fuchses, who moved to 366 South Second
Street, between Hooper and Keap. Daniel Fuchs was five years old
when he came to the place that was to become the wellspring of his
creative imagination and the greatest influence on his fictional
output.

The Williamsburg of Fuchs's youth was ethnically mixed. Later
there would be a more substantial Jewish migration, but in 1914 the
area was true "melting pot" New York. Fuchs's block was Jewish, but
the area itself was parceled off into sections, each with its own ethnic
group. The young children formed gangs, both for adventure and for
protection. Fuchs describes his block as a kind of island surrounded
by hostile ethnic gangs: the Irish down by the docks, the Italians in
Greenpoint, the Poles and Norwegians in the Bushwick area, the
Anglo-Saxons nearby on Hooper and Keap, the last tolerant for the
most part, except when they got drunk and murderous.[7] In one of his
earliest published pieces, Fuchs described this situation:

The district as I knew it in my boyhood was still comparatively free of serious
crime. . . . At this stage rough-house was mainly semi-pastime in nature,
providing a kind of sporting *gradus honorum* for all red-blooded youths. But
boy gangsters grew up into men, the East Side influence was strong, and
hooliganism became in one generation a business colorlessly operated by
many of the very individuals for whom it had been a boyish sport.[8]

The neighborhoods were rough and one had to learn the rules to
survive: Fuchs's tenement house contained a brothel or two at
various times, and his brother Rupert, during prohibition times,
worked—legitimately—on the speedboats of rum-runners operating

out of Sheepshead Bay or on the laundry trucks which, it was believed, were owned by people like Vannie Higgins.[9]

At the time of the move to Williamsburg, Fuchs's father set himself up in a new business. The city was putting up the Whitehall Building at 17 Battery Place, and there Jacob Fuchs started selling newspapers to the workers. When the building was completed he was given a concession stand, where he sold newspapers, candy, and magazines. The business branched out and he also sold papers to some of the steamship lines, the Whitehall Club, and the German consulate. During Christmastime the rich men who worked in the office building where he was located would give him orders for five-pound boxes of candy to be delivered to various parts of the city.[10] Daniel would sometimes go along on these trips, and it was then that he began to see that there was a world beyond his Williamsburg, which he described later as a "closed-in canyon."[11]

But for young Daniel Fuchs the world began to open up not so much through walks with his father as through books and the movies. Within a short distance of the street where he lived "there were no fewer than seven movie theatres." The programs were changed regularly and Fuchs went to the movies at least twice a week, sometimes more often than that. More than a way to become Americanized and educated, the movies provided for Fuchs and for many like him an escape from the world of Williamsburg:

. . . what these pictures did—with their virility and vigor, their command of life and consistently positive statements—was to act against the fear that possessed and constricted us.[12]

This fear, transferred from the parents to the children, was the lasting effect of the oppression of the Old World and of the hardships of adjusting to the new. Combined with the narrowness of the environment, such anxiety colored the psyche, clouding the horizon and closing it in. Fuchs wrote that on his block "you hardly saw the sky and seldom noticed the stars."[13] The movies enabled Daniel Fuchs to discover the stars and to dream of reaching them someday. The experience of the movies plays a central role in Fuchs's fiction, having shaped his style, his attitudes, and his vision.

Fiction, too, was a means of escape, and Fuchs recalls that he read "as one ate or breathed."[14] His father brought home magazines from his newsstand and Daniel read them: *Punch*, the *Tattler*, *Simplicissimus*, *Life*, *Judge*, and the *American Mercury*.[15] Novels, however, were his first love, and he read them avidly. He especially liked the "poor boy" English novelists, Lawrence and Maugham, but he admired Thackeray, Dickens, Chekhov, Gide, Huxley, and Joyce (*Dubliners* was a special favorite). Speaking about his youth today, he recalls knowing more about *Chrome Yellow* and *Antic Hay* than he knew about what was going on in Williamsburg: "A lot of my friends on the block were experts on Joyce and Proust, knew everything about Henry James. They wore the same pair of socks for a week, but they could tell you about the finest points in *Dubliners* and *Ulysses*."[16]

His literary bent displayed itself early; Fuchs remembers writing in elementary school. He was editor-in-chief of the *Eastern District High School Daisy* in Williamsburg. In this capacity the young editor unconsciously plagiarized pieces and styles from the *New Yorker* (then an exciting new publication), taking the "Talk of the Town" column and turning it into "Around the School."[17]

Later, at City College, Fuchs remained active in literary affairs, writing for and eventually editing the college's literary magazine, the *Lavender*. Some pieces dealing with his biology class and impressions of the college, which he had written for this magazine in imitation of the style of *transition* magazine, offended the chairman of the English department (Fuchs was originally an English major), and he was thrown out of that department. The kindness of a philosophy professor who happened to overhear the tale of this misfortune allowed him to enter the department of philosophy, which was his major when he graduated in 1930.

During his college years Fuchs spent his summers in camps in New England, serving as a Red Cross swimming examiner and instructor. At one of these camps in Pittsfield, Massachusetts, he met Susan Chessen, a junior counselor, and they were married in 1932.

A year earlier Fuchs had received his first real literary encouragement. He had sent to Malcom Cowley, then editor of the *New Republic*, a piece called "A Brooklyn Boyhood." Cowley was very impressed, printed part of it as "Where Al Capone Grew Up" (September 9, 1931), and recommended that Fuchs expand the account into a novel.[18]

Writing required time and leisure which Fuchs did not have. After graduating from college he taught as a permanent substitute at P.S. 225 in Brighton Beach. During the difficult times of the 1930s, teaching was the only job open to many educated people, and Fuchs recalls that the staff at P.S. 225 included many exceptionally bright and energetic people. The principal, Sol Branower, Fuchs still considers the "most brilliant man I have ever met," and he ran the school "beautifully."[19]

In the summer of 1932, freed from teaching, Fuchs and his new bride rented half a cottage in Woods Hole, Massachusetts. There Fuchs expanded "A Brooklyn Boyhood" into his first novel, *Summer in Williamsburg*. Remembering the experience of writing that first novel, he once wrote:

Summer in Williamsburg was written in a state of sheer terror. I didn't understand what I was doing and had read somewhere that authors often wrote books not understanding what they were writing but hoping that the reader would. That is really as it should be and no offense. But I didn't know it then. I was determined to write fairly. I wanted to be like the man from Mars. I wanted to examine everything with an absolutely clear view, unencumbered and unaffected.[20]

Next came the search for a publisher. Fuchs originally gave the manuscript to Simon and Schuster, where Clifton Fadiman, then a young editor there, held it for a long time and finally was forced to return it, with a memo reading "Won't sell." Then it went to Macmillan, whose editor Samuel Putnam liked it but was overruled by other members of the editorial staff, and the book was rejected. Finally accepted by Vanguard, which at that time was also publishing the work of James T. Farrell, *Summer in Williamsburg* appeared in 1934.[21] The novel was generally well received, but it did not inspire much enthusiasm among the critics.

Two years later, in 1936, Fuchs's second novel, *Homage to Blenholt*, appeared. Written in Connecticut in six weeks during a summer break from teaching, this novel was lighter in tone and more tightly structured than its predecessor. Typical of its more enthusiastic critical reception were the words of the *New York Times*'s critic: "*Homage to Blenholt* records a talent of strong portent. The date of Daniel Fuchs's next novel should appear in red on the calendar."[22]

The last novel he was to write for many years, *Low Company*, appeared the following year. Like the previous novels it was written during a summer vacation, this time at Yaddo, the artists' colony in the Berkshires. The reviews again were good but, in Fuchs's words, scant and immaterial."[23] The novels sold no more than about 2,000 copies altogether. Fuchs was angry, discouraged, and poor.

Soon, however, a new kind of job came his way. In 1937 he was

offered a contract by RKO to come to Hollywood to work on screenplays for thirteen weeks. But Hollywood was a Kafkaesque jungle of
the absurd for the young Fuchs. Quality work was discouraged and
there were even periods when he was paid hundreds of dollars a week
for doing nothing. He kept a diary while he was there, and from it
later published two short anti-Hollywood pieces, "Dream City or the
Drugged Lake" (1937) and "Hollywood Diary" (1938). After three
months he returned to New York.

At this point Fuchs "decided to become rich." He broke up a fourth
novel he was working on, called *Love in Brooklyn*, and turned it into
a number of short stories which he submitted to various magazines.
After a summer of waiting, all at once the acceptances came pouring
in:

Suddenly I heard from my agent. The editors had simply been away on their
summer vacations, that was all. They took the stories, all of them—one
afternoon three acceptances in the same mail. I had my race-track winnings
in cash all over me in different pockets; I had checks from the magazines laid
away in envelopes. The stories began to appear.[24]

In 1940 MGM bought the rights to film one of Fuchs's stories, "The
Fabulous Rubio," and called him out to work on it. That film was
never made, but this time Daniel Fuchs remained in Hollywood. He
would spend the next thirty years of his life writing for the movies.

Business in Hollywood was interrupted by World War II. Fuchs
remained in the states serving as an OSS enlisted man in the navy,
mostly in Washington, where his commanding officer was John
Ford.[25] Leaving the service in 1945, he returned to Hollywood.

Fuchs enjoyed a successful career as a screenwriter. In one of his
earliest assignments he was teamed with William Faulkner to work
on the screenplay of *Background to Danger*. Fuchs, in awe of the
great writer, had an uncomfortable relationship with him:

"I know why you don't cozy to me," he said softly to me one day, seeing that
things were going badly. "You don't cozy to me because you think I'm
anti-Semitic."
"Yes," I said. I was dismayed to hear myself saying, "How about that?"
"Well, it's troo-oo," he said, searching within himself and perplexed. "I
don't like Jews—but I don't like gentiles either."[26]

Neither Fuchs nor Faulkner received screen credit for the film.

Fuchs's first credited screenplay, *The Big Shot,* which starred Humphrey Bogart, was well received, and his next film, *The Hard Way,* an even bigger financial success, established him as a screenwriter. Over the years Fuchs wrote screenplays for a number of successful films, including *Panic in the Streets, Criss Cross,* and *Interlude.* In 1955 his screenplay for the film *Love Me or Leave Me* earned him an Academy Award. Fuchs also served on the Board of the Screen Writers' Guild for a number of years and then later went to England to work on film scripts, though none of these was ever filmed.

Daniel Fuchs is presently living in Los Angeles with his wife, still writing, and "working very happily."[27]

I Art Is a Class Weapon

The 1930s, the time of Fuchs's coming to artistic maturity, were years of upheaval, a time of fear, pain, disillusionment, and misery. Widespread unemployment, the downfall of governments, and the new threats of Nazism and Fascism contributed to an atmosphere of disillusionment that was all the more pronounced for its contrast to the previous decade.

The 1920s had been a time of economic expansion and well-being. Great technological progress was made, and businesses as well as individuals accumulated huge financial rewards. Although that decade witnessed a great deal of economic upheaval (technology made many people jobless), it was dominated by a spirit of optimism and hope. Many of the intellectuals, writers, and artists, however, did not share this feeling. To them, the spirit of people like Sinclair Lewis's Babbitt was disgraceful and the 1920s was a corrupt time. Perhaps T. S. Eliot's *The Waste Land* summed up the artist's attitude as well as any one work of that period. But while Eliot's poem expressed an attitude, the poem itself, in the difficulty of its style and content, embodied the deficiency inherent in the artist's reaction to his time.

Edmund Wilson, in his compassionate but critical study of writers of the 1920s, *Axel's Castle,* points out this deficiency, the prime sin of the artist. Running through the works of such writers as Gertrude Stein, Joyce, Proust, and Eliot was a series of common attitudes and ideas arising from a reaction to the rise of the middle class: believing that it was futile and foolish to oppose bourgeois power, they chose to exile themselves from society and social commitment and to withdraw into a private world. For these people, who became known as the Symbolists, art itself was an object of veneration, and reality became whatever the artist chose to see or experience. Wilson criticized the artist for using his art not to analyze and discuss the social life of his time, but, to borrow Michael Gold's phrase, to "masturbate" over the unique personality of the artist. The writer's sin was that he dropped out and offered his public little moral guidance. Implicit in Wilson's criticism of these writers was the conviction that "literature is something more than a cloister in a circus."[28] In "preferring one's absurdist chimeras to the most astonishing contemporary realities" these artists abandoned their responsibilities by "leaving the twentieth century behind."[29]

Malcolm Cowley offered a similar criticism of the artist of the 1920s in *Exiles Return.* An autobiographical account of his own experiences in the expatriate movement, this book also criticized his colleagues' personal and private approach to art and life. Cowley's experiences in the 1920s taught him that artists and art were impotent when they remained outside society and that the artistic rebellion must be rooted in political action.

The stock market crash and the resulting Depression, while putting an end to the hopes of progress that had characterized the 1920s, also opened up new avenues for the artist and the intellectual. As the unemployment lines grew longer and the middle class began to merge with the unemployed, the writer discovered that he had found a group and a society that he could associate with and become part of—the dispossessed and the disinherited. Richard Pells astutely comments that the greatest gift of the writer of the 1930s was the "sense of belonging."[30] The Depression gave the writer a chance to reestablish communication with his public (the dense literary style of the 1920s having alienated the writer from a wide audience), to join a movement which transcended the individual, and to find a viable outlet for his talent and creative output.

The need on the part of the writer to become involved in the class struggle produced the characteristic literature of the 1930s, a litera-ture primarily concerned with social issues and ways to transform society. The writer felt obligated to depict the plight of the masses and, through his work, to join the class struggle. This kind of art came to be called "proletarian." Perhaps the most famous proletarian literary critic is Granville Hicks, whose most famous work, *The Great Tradition,* outlined the necessary social arena of the novel of the future. His attitudes are typical of socially oriented critics:

It has become increasingly clear, even to those who do not want to see, that the central fact in American life is the class struggle. The writer has a series of choices. If he ignores the class struggle, he surrenders all hope of arriving at a clear interpretation, out of which a significant formal pattern may be devised, and he commits himself to evasion after evasion.[31]

Hicks, who criticized those writers who he felt avoided the social issues of their time and instead turned inward, attacked all of America's most distinguished writers. Hawthorne, Melville, Poe, James, Twain, and Faulkner were condemned for being more interested in their art than in the issues of their times. Even socially conscious writers like Howells, Dreiser, Sinclair, and Anderson were attacked; Hicks acknowledged that these writers portrayed life realistically, but he felt that their works suffered from a general incoherence and from inadequately conceived philosophies. Among the writers of the 1930s Hicks found his ideal in John Dos Passos. Here was a writer who held a Marxist point of view and dealt with American life accurately, emphasizing the class struggle.

Related to the radical and realist aesthetic espoused by Hicks were Michael Gold's views on proletarian realism. Gold, a longtime editor of the *New Masses* and one of the most influential critics of the new literature, outlined his aesthetic in a seminal essay, "Proletarian Realism":

1) Because the Workers are skilled machinists, sailors, farmers and weavers, the proletarian writer must describe their work with technical precision. . . .
2) Proletarian realism deals with the real conflicts of men and women who work for a living. It has nothing to do with the sickly mental states of the idle Bohemians, their subtleties, their sentimentalities, their fine spun affairs. The worst example and the best of what we do not want to do is the spectacle of Proust, master-masturbator of the bourgeois literature. . . .
3) Proletarian realism is never pointless. It does not believe in literature for its own sake, but in literature that is useful, has a social function. . . .[32]

Clearly tied to Gold's views was his belief that the majority of readers would be working-class people; as a result he insisted on simplicity of form and content. Because of the increasing popularity of the movies, radio, and film magazines, Gold insisted that writers should compete with popular culture.

During the meeting of the first American Writers Conference in 1935, many of these ideas were brought together. The concept of the proletarian novel was one of the main topics of discussion. The chairman of the conference, Waldo Frank, formally defined the term:

The term "proletarian" applied to art should refer to the key and vision in which the work is conceived, rather than the subject. It should be a qualitative, not quantitative, term. A story of middle class or intellectual life, or even of mythological figures, if it is alight with revolutionary vision, is more effective proletarian art—and more effective art for proletarians—than a shelfful of dull novels about stereotyped workers.[33]

The "proletarian novel" was then a fiction permeated with ideology, dedicated to promoting and advocating the ideas of the Communist party.

Fuchs stands out among the writers of his time as one of the few who did not write "doctrine" literature. None of Fuchs's novels takes socialism very seriously. The subject is raised in the first two novels, but only as an object of ridicule. Cohen, the *schlemiel*-like character of *Summer in Williamsburg*, decides to join the party in order to pursue a girl who is a party member. Having, in his own romantic-hysterical way, become excited by the party's ideals, he nevertheless abandons them in disgust when the girl refuses to sleep with him. Cohen then angrily denounces the party to his friend Philip:

. . . humanitarian effort is concerned with unimportant things. It's an expression of sentimentality. Let's suppose the Party is successful and all social ideals have been reached. What happens then? A man has enough to eat and drink, and he has a place to sleep in. That takes care of his physical wants and goes no further. You may say that this stage, the Utopia, has not been reached and won't be for a long time, that there is so much good yet to do. Well, why should I excite myself doing something that is essentially unimportant? These people in the party all give themselves, they have a wild full time with themselves, because it takes up all their energy and they are seriously occupied. But it has no meaning.[34]

The disenchantment expressed here (this is certainly Fuchs speaking) springs from a Dostoevskian distrust of human nature. Yes, the physical wants will be taken care of—but what about the spiritual? Fuchs does not offer solutions to such social problems. There are none.

This is not to say that Fuchs did not criticize the system. There is in his writing an implied criticism of capitalism. (Edward Dahlberg called this kind of writing "implication literature.") Fuchs's world is full of corruption and violence, and he demonstrates repeatedly that one must be dishonest and corrupt to succeed. One of the subplots of *Summer in Williamsburg* involves a warlike rivalry between two Williamsburg-based bus lines. The sections of the novel dealing with this story are filled with violence (breaking up of terminals, offices, and buses), bribery, and murder. The novel's final words, spoken by a gangster victorious in this power struggle, are ironic reminders of Fuchs's view of success in America:

"America," he repeated with conviction through the smoke, "I don't care what anybody says, America is a wonderful country. Seriously, seriously, I mean it. Look at me, look how I worked myself up in four short years. In America everyone has an equal chance. I don't know how things are in Russia now, even God himself don't know what's going on there these days, but even so, where, I want to know, where in the world could a Jew make such a man of himself as right here in America?"[35]

It is wrong, however, to emphasize too strongly the social strain in Fuchs, for, as David Madden says, "Fuchs wrote out of a private vision rather than a social consciousness and thus achieved art."[36] His themes go beyond the Depression, and his people are in many ways different even from those created by his Jewish contemporaries. Discussing Fuchs in comparison with Henry Roth, Walter Allen writes: "Fuchs' great theme is frustration, its comedy and pathos, frustration as an inescapable fact of life, not simply as a consequence of economic depression."[37] This frustration has a direct influence in Fuchs's fiction, generating the major themes of his early work, escape and entrapment, as well as the bleak outlook that darkens his vision. Unlike the hysterical self-pity and preaching that marked many of the "proletarian novels" of the time, however, Fuchs does not seek to change or overthrow or blame anyone, except perhaps God. He observes his people trying to live, making what they can of their lives. And if his people fail, if the vision is tragic, then that, for him, is reality.

This is not to say that Fuchs stood alone amidst a politically conscious intelligentsia. A number of prominent intellectuals opposed the proletarian philosophy and its exponents. Like Fuchs, Joseph Wood Krutch, drama critic for the *Nation*, did not believe that change was possible through art or politics. His essays on the function of literature reveal an attitude that Fuchs puts into practice in his fiction. In discussing Krutch's philosophy, Richard Pells points out:

For him, the supreme responsibility of art was to make life a bit more
tolerable by accepting the world as inherently imperfect and by describing it
accurately without extending the hope of some utopian improvement in the
future.[38]

Allen Tate, like Krutch, believed that the Communist critics were
distorting the basic realities of human experience. In a series of essays
written for the *New Republic,* Tate criticized the proletarian position
as too easy and untrue to the realities of life. For Tate, great poetry
always rejected the "easy solutions." In a later essay Tate declared
that the most perfect poetry (work of art) sought to "prove nothing,"
but created "the totality of experience in its quality; and it has no
useful relation to the ordinary forms of action."[39] For Tate, then, it
was the duty of the artist to reflect and record the basic, essential,
unchanging facts and truths about man and his world—to see life in its
"totality."

Fuchs's philosophy of art is in keeping with that of Tate and Krutch.
Certainly his work is an attempt to come to grips with the essential
unchanging truths about man and his surroundings. If the truth about
life is that it is sad and cold and that man, limited by his flesh, cannot
really contend with it—so be it. Fuchs's occasional anger is understandable, but his work is a record of acceptance, an acknowledgment of life as it is and always was. His vision is sad but wisely
resigned to the truth of experience.

His contemporary, Albert Halper, a Jew who came from a similar
background but who wrote socially conscious novels, wrote of him:
"Daniel Fuchs is a man with a heavy burden. He has a burden almost
as heavy as Dostoevsky. I do not envy him. . . . Fuchs is a child of
sorrow."[40] This sorrow transcends time and makes the themes of
Fuchs's novels accessible and pertinent to all men in all times. It has
its roots, however, in the *shtetl* of the nineteenth-century East
European Jew. Here is where his real ancestry can be found, and it is
within these villages that one must look to gain an even better
understanding of Daniel Fuchs.

II   *The Yiddish Influence*

Major characteristics of classic Yiddish fiction, a literature that
came into its own in the late nineteenth century, often emerge in
Fuchs's work, especially in the first two novels. He shapes such

material, however, for his own purposes: at times he utilizes conventions only to turn them inside out; occasionally he destroys them.

Whether or not Fuchs read Yiddish literature, the Williamsburg he grew up in was full of the kinds of people who populate Yiddish fiction. He must have been friendly with people who could tell him stories and expose him to Jewish culture. Mr. Balkan, the father of the hero of *Homage to Blenholt*, usually resorts to burying himself in his Yiddish paper to escape the nagging of his wife, and on a number of occasions he refers to the "Bintel Brief," an advice column by the editor of the *Jewish Daily Forward*. This paper and others were to be found in the Fuchs home, constituting an important cultural experience for the boy. During the years of Fuchs's youth the Yiddish press was instrumental in bringing to American audiences the literature of such distinguished writers as Sholom Aleichem, Sholom Asch, and Isaac Loeb Peretz.[41]

Living in a Jewish community composed mainly of transported and relocated European Jews enabled Fuchs to absorb the Yiddish culture, and his writing probably represents the truest and most fully realized picture of immigrant Jewish life in America. Allen Guttman writes: "Daniel Fuchs was the first to take apart the world of Sholom Aleichem's Kasrilevka and to reconstruct it on the sidewalks of New York."[42] The reference to Sholom Aleichem, the most famous of Yiddish writers, provides a good starting point for a consideration of some of the important aspects of Yiddish writing.

The culture of the East European Jews was a culture in exile. The *Golus* (exile, a word used extensively by Fuchs) was the term used to embody the sense of homelessness. The Jews were a people with no homeland, a community continually denied dignity, respect, or a secure place among their fellow human beings. They lived under the difficult irony of being taught that they were the chosen people of God, yet experiencing in their lifetime only the pain of rejection, the despair of a people with no rights, nation, or friends. Despite, or perhaps because of, the conditions and attitudes of the outside world, the Jews of Eastern Europe were a cohesive and unified group. They were held together by strong religious and spiritual ties and a sense of destiny.

Perhaps the central characteristic of the Jewish people and their literature is the belief in the perfectability of life. The Jew totters between the mundane reality of life and the ideal world which exists somewhere within the real world; his great hope is to create the New

Jerusalem in the here-and-now. John Clayton refers to the attitude as "Heaven is the world redeemed."[43] Mendele Mocher Seforim, considered the father of Yiddish literature, commented:

> The life of the Jews, although it seems outwardly ugly and dark in color, is inwardly beautiful; a mighty spirit animates it, the divine breath which flutters through it from time to time. . . . Israel is the Diogenes of the nations; while his head towers in the heavens and is occupied with deep meditation concerning God and his wonders, he himself lives in a barrel. . . .[44]

The most painful aspect of Fuchs's work (especially the "Williamsburg novels") is his inability to foresee such redemption in this life, and this failure sets him apart from most Jewish writers. When reading the novels in progression, one can sense Fuchs's soul-struggle to keep some dream, some hope, alive. Even in his most damning study, *Low Company*, when all seems to be abandoned, in a book so filled with excruciating gloom, he pauses for at least one more look back (like Abraham, he will plead for Sodom to be saved if at least one good man can be found):

> He had known the people at Ann's in their lowness and had been repelled by them, but now it seemed to him that he understood how their evil appeared in their impoverished dingy lives and further, how miserable their own evil rendered them. It was not enough to call them low and pass on.[45]

Fuchs, unfortunately, did pass on. He stopped writing novels for thirty-four years. His was resignation—passive, hopeless, tortured. Among American Jewish writers this attitude is unusual; only Fuchs's contemporary Nathanael West echoes this wounded negativism.

Fuchs explores the misery of life with great care and in detail, as did Yiddish writers of the past, whose stories are full of life's pain and suffering. But while they take a long and complete look at the worst, they do hold out hope for man; the hero usually manages to triumph in some way. Fuchs's stories, again, do not take this upswing, but his tone of compassion reconnects him with his Yiddish ancestors. This compassion goes hand in hand with his vision of constriction and silence. Unlike his contemporaries, whose lashing out at the system that had betrayed them was full of moral indignation and hate, Fuchs's tone is sympathetic and often even playful. One reviewer pointed this out as a distinguishing characteristic of Fuchs's work:

Here is more than the compassion so glibly accredited to many novelists who lead their amiable characters through deep vales of suffering; here is an almost Dostoevskian capacity to pity and forgive the unamiable, futile and evil characters that people his world. Farrell hates humanity, hates the forces that have made it what it is, and seeks to annihilate the present order by holding up to it its own hideous image. Fuchs, however, loves humanity, accepts the forces that have made it, and seeks to comfort it with self-knowledge.[46]

Fuchs does indeed love his people despite their weaknesses, despite their sins. This makes his outrage all the more painful and tortured. And there is outrage. His early fiction depicts a universe that is rigged against a poor, helpless mankind (merely flesh and blood) that is not mentally or physically equipped to deal with this world or with a God who at best no longer cares about its predicament.

The Jews of the early Yiddish writers also lived in a difficult and, more often than not, terrifying world, but their attitudes toward life, and especially toward God, were never this angry. The Jews' relationship to God, writes Irving Howe, was "social, intimate and critical." The God to whom the Yiddish writers spoke "had been humanized and taught the uses of mercy."[47] Sholom Aleichem uses this device most effectively in his "Tevye stories," where Tevye does not hesitate to criticize God. The fact that affairs have been apparently mismanaged cannot be ignored. (There is a famous Yiddish story of a group of rabbis who brought God to trial and found him guilty of mismanagement.) Tevye realizes this but takes comfort in his faith, feeling that all eventually will turn out for the best: "And, in any case, you simply cannot leave God out of the reckoning. You cannot ignore his Torah and the long line of generations which have died to keep it alive."[48] Irving Howe writes:

Tevye represents the generation of Jews that could no longer find complete deliverance in the traditional God yet could not conceive of abandoning him. No choice remained, therefore, but to celebrate the earthly condition: poverty and hope.[49]

Rather than reasserting this cycle of criticism and reaffirmed faith, Fuchs simply implies that God is guilty and leaves it at that. God is guilty because He has apparently lost interest. In Fuchs's universe there is no traditional faith to fall back on. His characters have already abandoned the religion of their ancestors, and tradition and ritual no longer have any meaning. What remains is the pity and the compassion. Fuchs, the author, gives his people what God does not—love.

However, Fuchs, especially in the early fiction, did not cast his themes in a tragic light. His work is often very funny and his attitude comic. Howard Moss, writing on the "Williamsburg novels," remarks:

To see humiliation from a comic viewpoint is rare. It is less a matter of self-knowledge and dispassion than of temperament. The slum life of Brooklyn Jews, a life of poverty and debasement, is anything but intrinsically funny, and from a social viewpoint it is tragic. It is the particular triumph of Daniel Fuchs that in three novels written on the subject in the thirties . . . his characters are neither too charming nor too heroic. Moreover, they are often marvelously funny.[50]

Humor is a distinguishing aspect of Jewish fiction. It was and is used as a defense, protecting the Jew from the harshness of life about him. Irving Howe has written:

Only if they took the myth of the Chosen People with the utmost seriousness, yet simultaneously mocked their pretensions to being anything but the most wretched people on earth, could the Jews survive.[51]

The basic tenor of Jewish humor is closely bound up in the character of the *schlemiel*, the most famous type in Yiddish fiction. Ruth Wisse, in her study of the *schlemiel*, writes:

. . . The impulse . . . of schlemiel literature in general, is to use this comical stance as a stage from which to challenge the political and philosophical status-quo.[52]

Max Balkan, the most fully realized *schlemiel* character in Fuchs's fiction, makes this challenge directly:

In all great classical works, what made them classics was the distinguishing characteristic of heroism and nobility. In those days people lived with richness and glory. These qualities were gone in America in 1935, it was true, but to him it seemed like an enormous pity. He wanted to say that he meant to look for heroism in his own life, to live with meaning and vigor, ridiculous and painful as this search might make him feel at times.[53]

Most important, the *schlemiel* always retains a sense of his unique self. No onslaughts from reality or "slings and arrows" of fortune shake this sense of identity. As Professor Wisse states, "The schlemiel represents the triumph of identity despite the failure of circumstance."[54]

Fuchs's *schlemiels* exhibit all of these characteristics, but in the end no victory, real or psychological, is achieved. They become victims, are cheated or destroyed, or even killed. In keeping with his refusal to credit easy solutions or social panaceas, Fuchs avoids the traditional happy ending that would falsify his vision.

The emphasis in Jewish writing on the *schlemiel* character is closely related to the stress placed upon the theme of antiheroism. Classical Jewish writers have tended to admire not the great overreachers of tragedy but those able to live and endure in silence. Tevye the dairyman is the classic example of this type. He, according to Irving Howe, is the "anti-heroic Jewish hero whose sheer power of survival and comment makes the gesture of traditional heroism seem rather absurd."[55] The little man (Dos Kleine Menschele), the poor but proud householder trying to maintain some kind of status in the world as he continually grows poorer, appeals to the sensibility of the Jewish writer. "Any one they seem to say can learn to conquer the world but only a Tevye, or a literary descendent of Tevye can learn to live in it."[56]

Fuchs's two most lovable characters, and two he obviously admires, the fathers of the protagonists of his first two novels, Mr. Hayman and Mr. Balkan, exhibit these qualities and the moral resolution that must support them. Both men have learned to live with dignity, to be honest, loving, compassionate, and good. Both have chosen to retain their principles and their ideals rather than to trade them for the financial success that others around them enjoy and that tempts their sons to seek lesser, gaudier heroes. Fuchs loves these people. This love for what they are, and his increasing awareness that such a life in today's world only produces impotence and failure seem to be the overriding reasons for his disgust, his wound, and his resignation.

Fuchs's imagination was shaped more by his childhood and adolescent experiences than by the 1930s. The Yiddish tradition was closely bound up with those memories. By exorcising those memories and utilizing certain traditions, he forged a private but universal vision.

III *Fuchs and Nathanael West*

Fuchs's novels, as has been shown, do not fit comfortably into any of the "proletarian" categories. In this independence of vision, so unusual in the 1930s, his work is allied to that of his contemporary, Nathanael West. There are certain surface similarities: both were born in New York City of immigrant Jewish parents, and each wrote four novels (though Fuchs may yet write more) and worked in Hollywood. West, however, did not come from Williamsburg, nor did the world of his youth even remotely resemble it. His father was a successful builder and was able to provide his son with an Ivy League college education (Brown), expensive clothes (Brooks Brothers suits), a trip to Paris, and other such luxuries of the wealthy.[57]

As writers, West and Fuchs differ radically in style. Ranging from the surrealistic and lyrical to the parodic, West's novels are short (except for *The Day of the Locust*) and sometimes explosive. Fuchs, on the other hand, writes traditional novels, realistic, rather lengthy, and filled with well-developed and three-dimensional characters. In a Fuchs story there is a definite sense of place, with recognizable and realistic settings, and plots that weave together two or more threads. West's characters are usually symbolic and sometimes flat; his settings range from the inside of the Trojan Horse (*The Dream Life of Balso Snell*) to the nightmare landscape of *Miss Lonelyhearts* to Wu Fong's House of All Nations (*A Cool Million*).

In the areas of temperament and vision, however, there are very marked similarities. One critic writes of West:

Unlike . . . so many of the current Jewish-American writers, West was unable to rest content in the human suspension between heavenly aspirations and earthly limitations, belief and skepticism, order and disorder. He portrays life in his novels as a conflict of inadequate imperatives offered to man by society and culture as guides to live by.[58]

West, like his crowd in *The Day of the Locust*, felt betrayed by life (the original title of that novel was *The Cheated*), and his sense of the fraudulence of life pervades all his novels. Victor Comerchero writes, "In a sense, he seems to have inherited that complex mixture of pride and metaphysical unworthiness that is a part of Jewish heritage."[59] *Miss Lonelyhearts*, for example, can conceive of himself as a Christ figure, one who will bring comfort to all of the "desperates" and "sick of it alls" of this world, but in the end is only capable of botched attempts and disillusionment. In the end he is accidentally killed, not deliberately crucified. Those who attempt to rise above the earth are doomed to find out that they are merely human, confined to a low and despicable state.

West's novels all center around various dreams, each dissecting its given dream and showing both the lies underneath it and man's inability to achieve it. Miss Lonelyhearts says, "Men have always fought their misery with dreams," and if *Balso Snell* presents the sham behind dreams of art, *Miss Lonelyhearts* presents the victims of it. To solve the problems of human misery Miss Lonelyhearts must resolve what amounts to an unsolvable contradiction. He seeks to transcend his human self by invoking the divine; but this too is illusory: being human, of course, means that he is anything but divine; this is the contradiction and the tragedy of life. The inability of man to merge these two strains is the underlying frustration of West (and of Fuchs). Unable to resolve the contradictions, men such as Miss Lonelyhearts can only escape into delusion and death.

The Day of the Locust is West's logical conclusion to the failure of the Christ dream. There is no redeemer. Tod Hackett, the character through whose eyes the action is seen, says "that he had never set himself up as a healer"; rather he refers to himself as a prophet of the coming destruction. Dreams as a form of escape are still dominant here, however. Faye Greener dreams of becoming a great actress, Harry Greener escapes into fantasies of being a fine comedian. Homer Simpson has no dreams—he sleeps to escape. Tod also dreams, but he is aware of the reasons, whereas the others are not.

California, the setting of the novel, is the home of the movies—the land of dreams. West's grotesques come here for a fulfillment of their dreams, but they find that the promised land is only another waste land:

Once there, they discover that sunshine isn't enough. . . . They haven't the mental equipment for leisure, the money for the physical equipment for pleasure. Did they slave so long just to go to an occasional Iowa picnic? What else is there?[60]

West's novel culminates in an apocalyptic burning of Los Angeles, in which the victims become the victimizers, "the inevitable vengeance of those who, cheated by life, find that even their dreams have destroyed them."[61]

Fuchs's characters, especially in the early novels, are also dreamers, ruined by life in various ways, for he, too, is preoccupied with the disparity between what man should be and what he actually is. As in West, the recognition of this dichotomy often leads Fuchs into comedy, which is unusual in the writing of the 1930s. His characters, also, are often unable to maintain the delicate balance between the two poles, to harmonize the reality that degrades them with the dreams that would ennoble them. Cohen, the *schlemiel*-like dreamer in *Summer in Williamsburg*, is a first cousin to Miss Lonelyhearts, trying to rise above the squalor that is his life by living in the imagination or the world of art. When this fails, he moves uncertainly toward social commitment. Like Miss Lonelyhearts, he bleeds for suffering mankind:

I remember something I once saw when I was a boy. . . . Once I saw a woman in the winter time walking past the tall iron railing slowly, weeping by herself. I shall never forget the image, the huge brick synagogue, the tall railings, the winter gray sky, and the way that poor woman wept. I knew it was real, no fake, some real heartache. [62]

Cohen finally discovers that he can do nothing and, even worse, that there is nothing to be done. The age has robbed man of his soul; there is no way to rise above the earth. For him, too, death is the only escape.

Max Balkan, the dreamer of *Homage to Blenholt*, lives in visions of power and glory. He resolves that his will not be a life of common labor but of executive action, thinking great ideas and controlling businesses all over the world. These are the dreams of those "who have come to California" in *The Day of the Locust*. They, too, chase the dream of glory. From Williamsburg to Olympus!

These are the dreams perpetuated by the movies, those molders of life and human aspiration which lie at the very heart of the work of both West and Fuchs. The film studios, dream factories, which produce the products that soothe the dull ache of the Depression, have manufactured the illusions that desperate souls are forced to cling to. The movies have cheapened men's dreams. They are a great lie in that they have debased the unhappiness of life. Max's dreams are, of course, never realized. Reality finally crushes him. He will end up, not as a tycoon, but as a part-owner of a delicatessen.

Low Company (1937) represents for its author a culmination; it was Fuchs's last word in the 1930s. Here the questlike nature of the earlier novels is replaced by a firm knowledge that reality cannot be sidestepped, but must be accepted. Unlike the earlier novels in which the characters' encounters with reality end in disillusionment, this novel deals with people who are already victims, and they know it. Gone is the humor of the earlier novels, displaced by a pervasive gloom. Neptune Beach is a grim wasteland of vice, corruption, and murder. Escaping misery is man's only goal. Prostitution is big business, and violence seems to be the chief occupation of the novel's characters. All are "low company" and remain in the gutter. Men are but men—life is still Williamsburg.

The final statement of both writers in the 1930s was one of defeat. West's work culminated in an apocalyptic vision of the end of the world, his final statement. A few months after the publication of *The Day of the Locust*, West was killed in an auto crash. Fuchs's statement was just as pessimistic, though not as dramatic. West's sensibility leaned toward the parable and the metaphor; Fuchs's realism did not allow him to indulge in such dramatics. His novels lack West's grand finales, because life possesses no real drama ("People do not live in dramatic situations"). People's lives at most may contain a number of minor climaxes; there is certainly no apocalypse.

In an era that produced writing that was almost always political in nature, Fuchs and West wrote books that are remarkably apolitical. They confronted a universe so decidedly rigged against man that any effort to contend with it leads only to absurdity. However, both of these writers were influenced by immediate social reality, and the Depression did leave its special mark on their writings. Certainly the works of these men display the shock and sense of despair brought on by the times. Political cures are not recommended; no solutions of any kind even seem possible in their stories, which is certainly atypical of American and Jewish literature and "almost un-American in its refusal to admit the possibility of improvement, amelioration or cure."[63] In the novels of West and Fuchs the Depression became a metaphor and was thus generalized into an image of universal human suffering:

"It is hard," West tells us . . . "to laugh at the need for beauty and romance, no matter how tasteless, even horrible, the results of that need are. But it is easy to sigh. Few things are sadder than the truly monstrous."[64]

Both writers deal with man's need for beauty and romance in what Fuchs describes as a "flat age." This need, this attempt of man to fulfill his desires, and the results and implications of this quest are at the heart of the fiction of both men. "The truly monstrous"—man's entrapment in a world where "flowers smelled of feet"—provoked

West's anger and despair; Daniel Fuchs's confusion, which began in anger, turned to tears, to a love for his fellow man, and finally to an acceptance of the overpowering force of reality.

CHAPTER 2

Life in the Raw

S*ummer in Williamsburg* begins as the oppressive heat of a New York City summer has momentarily given way to a rainstorm. The frantic activity and noise that characterize life in Williamsburg have ceased; for a brief time, at least, there is quiet. Suddenly a woman screams. It is Mrs. Sussman, whose husband, Meyer, the butcher, has placed a basketball bladder over his face and breathed gas.

Philip Hayman, a senior at City College, through whose eyes the action of the novel will be presented, is shocked and puzzled by this apparently senseless act. He decides to ask Old Miller ("Miller knew everything") to explain to him the reasons for the suicide. Miller's answer provides a clue to the novel's construction and purpose:

To find out properly you must first understand Meyer Sussman, and this, of course, is the most difficult thing to do. Even if I were God, I am afraid I might not be able to do this, there are so many persons. But even when you know Sussman you are only at the beginning of the problem, for then you must make a laboratory out of Williamsburg, to find out what touched him here, why these details affected him and in what manner. . . . If you would really discover the reason, you must pick Williamsburg to pieces until you have them spread out on your table before you, a dictionary of Williamsburg. And then select. Pick and discard. ... . Collect and then analyze to understand the quality of each detail. Perhaps then you might know why Sussman died, but granting everything I do not guarantee the process.[1]

Fuchs's first novel is a "dictionary of Williamsburg," written, according to one critic, as "a melange of contrapuntal scenes."[2] This observation correctly describes the form of Fuchs's narrative, but his complex technique might be more helpfully defined as cinematic. The movies are a powerful force in the lives of the people of Williamsburg, and Fuchs, who also saw many movies in his youth, seems to have been influenced by cinematic narrative devices. He

35

relies heavily upon dialogue, setting, and gestures, constructing the novel as a series of short scenes. Each scene presents an action and then dissolves, usually at a moment of great stress; then Fuchs cuts to another scene. Usually scenes follow each other as parallel pictures showing different people making attempts at love or heroism, or engaging in some violent activity. Often adjacent scenes tacitly comment on each other, as when scenes of organized underworld crime dissolve into scenes of children's gang fights.

The novel opens with a typical cinematic narrative device: a kind of panoramic view (long shot) that gives an overall picture of Williamsburg. Fuchs then changes to the closeup, presenting individual portraits of specific faces, emphasizing some members of the community. In compiling his picture of Williamsburg life, he enters the lives of nearly a dozen of these people, but focuses his attention on Philip Hayman, his family, and friends. By examining these lives he hopes to understand Williamsburg.

This novel, like Fuchs's other work, takes place in summer, that time of year when life is exposed, like the flesh of an unclothed person, when feelings and anxieties become sharpened as people crowd the streets to escape the oppressive heat of closed-in places. Philip senses the summer's peculiar harshness: he "longed for the winter because then life in Williamsburg grew less exposed, less crude, and a little gentle" (pp. 371–72).

Fuchs's people are poor, sweating, pained Jews who inhabit small claustrophobic apartments in tenements in a poor, squalid Jewish section of New York City. Only the wealthy are able to cushion themselves from life's harsh realities, because they have the means to surround themselves with ornaments, luxury items, and conveniences, which serve to brighten up life and disguise its emptiness. One sees less of it, because he allows as little as possible to crawl into his home. When he visits the home of a wealthy friend, Philip is forced to admit that "the texture of existence might be enriched by furniture, books and surroundings" (p. 196). Williamsburg, however, has no adornments. It is easy to explore life here, for nothing has to be pared away. Here one can see life in the raw. By studying Williamsburg, by putting this pure product under a microscope, perhaps life can be understood—perhaps questions (Philip's and Fuchs's) can be answered.

The novel is an attempt to understand Williamsburg and, by extension, life. "For him [Fuchs]," writes Irving Howe, "Williamsburg is the world."[3] At the beginning of the novel Old Miller tells Philip "that at bottom everything in the world was flat and common mud" (p. 9), a conclusion that is confirmed by Philip at the end of the novel. The lives depicted, the incidents related, add up to very little. Philip, looking out of his apartment window at a street scene below him, reflects:

These were people as God made them and as they were. They sat in the sunshine going through the stale operations of living, they were real, but a novelist did not write a book about them. No novel, no matter how seriously intentioned was real. . . . People did not live in dramatic situations. (pp. 375–76)

Fuchs, however, has written a novel which successfully captures the essence of this "stale operation of living." There is nothing grand or heroic about his characters, though some make absurd gestures in striving for glory. They do nothing, nor do they accomplish anything out of the ordinary. They live, breathe, sweat, and complain. Many endure, some die. There are a few happy moments and few genuinely sad ones. What occurs in between is routine—nothing to write a novel about. Yet Fuchs has written a novel about it, one that contains, in one critic's words, "a quantity of felt life."[4]

Summer in Williamsburg is the most personal of Fuchs's novels. It is closely tied to his young manhood, and in many ways it is an attempt to exorcise the ghosts of his past. Almost thirty years after the publication of the novel, Fuchs wrote about the terrible experience he had in producing his first book:

Everyone's adolescence is no doubt precious and important to him, but I don't think it was Williamsburg or my adolescence there which caused my terror; although years later, driving through Williamsburg, I found myself shaking all over. No, what caused my trouble was that I was trying to find a design. . . . I was trying to find a similar direction and plan to the life I had witnessed in Williamsburg. I was struggling with form. I was struggling with mystery.[5]

The "mystery" that Fuchs wrestles with is the elusive process of creating a work of art from the experience of life. The difficulty of his task must arise at least partially from the complexity of that life, from Williamsburg itself. The novel becomes an attempt to bring some kind of order to his experience there.

In many ways *Summer in Williamsburg* is closely related to the naturalist novels of the late nineteenth century. One of the major characteristics of the naturalist was his desire to seek the truth with a scientific objectivity. Emile Zola, often considered the father of naturalism, said, "We naturalists, we men of science, we must admit of nothing occult: men are but phenomena and the conditions of phenomena."[6] The need to explore life in all its details is reflected in Old Miller's advice to Philip. Later he echoes Zola: "The ultimate product, man, therefore moves mysteriously, but he is a scientific outcome of cause and effect" (p. 12). Philip attempts during the course of the novel to follow this advice in his desire to understand Williamsburg. Miller's dictum that man is a product of cause and effect is in keeping with the naturalistic credo that man is shaped by his environment. Certainly Williamsburg itself is the single most powerful force in the book.

Environment indeed determines the lives of the characters, but Fuchs's vision goes even deeper than this. Like many naturalists, Fuchs feels that the individual is wholly impotent in the face of a universe that is cruel or at best indifferent. In this, his first novel, Fuchs even includes God as a character, portraying Him as an onlooker, a detached observer, amused by the spectacle of His pathetic creations who scurry about trying to make something of themselves and their lives.

Such a God is very similar to the divinity in the poetry of Stephen Crane, whose brief verses starkly present an unapproachable, indifferent force:

> A man said to the universe:
> "Sir, I exist!"
> "However," replied the universe,
> "The fact has not created in me
> A sense of obligation."[7]

The universe's response is echoed in a scene at the end of Fuchs's novel. Philip Hayman and his friend Charlie Nagleman are on a train. A woman, trying to get off the train, is having difficulty because of the crowd:

"Lemme off," she cried to Charlie, "lemme off. This is my station. I want to get off."

"Nevertheless," Charlie said cooly, "the fact creates in me no sense of obligation."

"Crazy! Crazy!" she cried at him over her shoulder as they walked from the train. (p. 325)

The deliberate reference to Crane points to a similarity in viewpoint. The universe is a trap, rigged against man. His efforts to contend with it are as futile as his supplications to a deaf God. And the woman's response is appropriate; it is crazy.

The naturalist, according to V. L. Parrington, also displays a bias toward pessimism in selecting details.[8] The summer that Fuchs tells of is crowded with sordid occurrences: the novel chronicles three suicides, two deaths, one murder, three unhappy marriages, and gang wars played out by organized mobs and by young children. Fuchs depicts a world in which love is "a hot joke," where no poetry or heroism exists, and where violence and dishonesty are a way of life.

In certain sophisticated forms of naturalism, the individual is a victim, the butt of a sardonic cosmic joke; life is a trap. The theme of entrapment is central in all of Fuchs's fiction. In *Summer in Williamsburg* all of the characters and situations depicted illustrate various forms and aspects of entrapment. This is Fuchs's vision: to analyze it closely is to explore these traps—those that are imposed from without and those imposed from within.

I *Idealist in Extremis*

The character who most effectively symbolizes the longing for escape is Cohen, who is a friend of Philip and the only other male character of Philip's age in the Williamsburg community. He is an exaggerated version of Philip's romantic and poetic nature, that part of Philip which is at war with his practical side. Philip is too wise or too weary to give credence to Cohen's preposterous yowlings. An exchange between the two friends at the end of the novel points to the difference between them:

"Ferret?" Philip said. "Oh, no. I do not ferret, I see what I see. The whole point is I don't embellish what I see with false ornamentation. Once it is false it no longer interests me. I'm willing to accept beauty and romance when I find it, but there's no necessity for kidding myself about it."

"In that case you will never find it. This is something that does not exist by itself. The individual must have the vision. In short, Hayman, your wisdom is undergraduate and cynical." (p. 360)

Cohen is a dreamer, but a confused one. He will try anything to get out of this world. Reality is too strong a force, however, and Cohen finally learns that one cannot contend with it.

The relationship between the two friends is similar to the Miss Lonelyhearts–Shrike relationship in Nathanael West's *Miss Lonelyhearts*. Miss Lonelyhearts also has a tendency to glorify things, to conceive of things in unworldly terms; and Shrike is always there to remind him of the reality of life.[9] Philip, however, is no Shrike. He is not a complete cynic, nor is he hardened or deliberately cruel. He has a great affection for Cohen, though he strives to correct his errors of unrestricted imagination. Philip knows there is a touch of Cohen in him, but when he sees this side of himself being played out in real life by a real person, he is taken aback. When he reprimands Cohen, he is also reprimanding himself. In his reaction against this side of himself, Philip often serves as a foil to Cohen's attitudes and ideas.

Cohen is trapped in a kind of Purgatory. He lives in Williamsburg (Earth), which is presented as a kind of burning hell during the summer ("someone must have turned on the heat"), but he longs for a world of poetry, intellectual stimulation, and luxury. He is trapped between what he is ("He was ugly with his pimples. His hair was thin, and he had to oil it and plaster it over the bald spots.") and what he longs to be—a famous writer, a poet, an Adonis, a sophisticated man about town:

. . . Reality was too much for him. Unable to find some girl to love as they loved in the nineteenth century lyrics that Cohen memorized, Cohen lacked the energy and the confidence to avail himself of the pleasures to be found in Halper's stable lots, the cellars, or the roofs. The world confused him, frightened him, and he set upon improving it and transforming it to suit his fancy. (p. 266)

Thus he resembles E. A. Robinson's Miniver Cheevy, who, unable to duplicate "the medieval grace of iron clothing . . . kept on drinking." Cohen tries to escape too, but by living in the imagination rather than in the bottle. The similarity to Cheevy is marked, for like many of Robinson's people, Cohen is a dreamer of the ideal; or, to use Hyatt Waggoner's phrase, an "idealist in extremis."[10]

Sometimes his Miniver Cheevy quality expresses itself more literally, as he seeks to reinforce the intoxication of pure imagination. One evening during a party he gets drunk ("Cohen liked to fake drunkenness upon the least provocation"—an obvious escapist tactic). This time he isn't faking, though he does attempt to ennoble the effects:

"Have a drink." He swayed over to Philip. "It shuts the eye, Hayman, it destroys Gehenna, obliterates the Everlasting Nay and relieves the soul's torment." (p. 57)

He gets so drunk that he has to be carried out by some friends. When the effects of the liquor begin to wear off, Cohen finds himself in the subway, where he accidentally boards the wrong train and travels to Coney Island. Embarrassed by his drunken foolishness, he becomes furious with himself. He hears the noise of a carnival ride and contemplates suicide, recalling "a newspaper story about a woman who had stood up in the excitement of the ride and consequently smashed her head when she hit a beam above" (p. 71).

He buys a ticket and gets on the ride, but the reality of suicide is too much for him. Cohen can't bring himself to make that heroic gesture:

Cohen saw the beam before him. Stand up! he cried to himself, soon you will be passing the beam, the opportunity will be lost. Stand up! His mind, his spirit rose; his body was still sweating on the wooden seat. (p. 72)

This last sentence neatly captures one of the major themes in Fuchs's work, the gaping chasm between the spirit and the flesh. Flesh rots, it sweats, it stinks, it gets in the way of the ideal and the yearnings of the spirit.

His attempt at suicide a failure, he must find another release for his pent-up emotions, and he finds it in violence. In the work of a writer like West (*The Day of the Locust*) this kind of violence, which results from frustration, takes on horrifying implications, as it will in Fuchs's later work. In the case of Cohen, however, it only emphasizes the pathetic ineptness of his character. Seeing a fight taking place on the beach, he rushes into the fray. One of the fighters hits him over the head, however, and knocks him out. Even this kind of passive action is something, and Cohen is content: "When he arose he felt singularly cold and satisfied."

The next sustained section of the novel dealing with Cohen also culminates in a suicide attempt. Once again he tries to rise above the earth, and once again reality asserts itself. Cohen, who has always been singularly unsuccessful with girls, finally manages to get a date; he is to escort a girl to the wedding reception for Tessie, a neighborhood girl who is a close friend of Philip's. As befits his unfortunate physical appearance, however, Cohen finds himself unable to cope with women: "It was like walking on eggs." Ruffled by his date's icy manner, he accidentally steps onto the wrong train. The

girl, to his embarrassment, makes him aware of his error and tells him
to get off, but Cohen hesitates, and the doors close on him. The scene
is pathetic but comic. Here his plight is laughable, though later the
tone will change. Like the *schlemiel* he is, Cohen will try to raise
himself above the situation, figuring that there is yet time to redeem
himself, and left alone in the train, he can dream of an idealized
evening to come:

There would be potted palms and soft music. Lovely ladies, each looking like
a different flower, would sigh at him because he was so unapproachable. . . .
As the train beat the rails Cohen took heart. The evening was just beginning.
(p. 150)

At the party Cohen's date ignores him, but he has a good time
nonetheless, for he finds a group of girls willing to listen and
appreciate his anecdotes. Soon "he was feeling brilliant, suave, and
self-assured." But his buoyant mood cannot last, and when Tessie's
father finds that he has left the pickled herring at home, Cohen
volunteers to retrieve it, telling himself that he cuts a "gallant and
dashing" figure in so boldly setting out to rescue the situation. He is
now completely lost in his unreal world. His frame of mind is such
that he even decides to take a cab to bring him and the jar of herring
back to the reception hall. Inevitably, his "flesh" reasserts itself:

As they came to the wedding hall Cohen opened the door while the cab was
still in motion. He bounced out and worked snappily on the brown-and-white
jar. His hand slipped, the jar fell to the sidewalk, the pickled fish slipping
over Cohen's trousers and sliding onto the ground. Cohen smelled the
overpowering stench of herring all over him . . . He was just beginning to
have a good time, he had been so happy and exultant, that wonderful mood
had passed already and it all came back. He almost wept from disappointment
and misery. What could he do about the tuxedo? It was stained and ruined,
the man who rented them would demand full payment for it. Cohen's heart
ached with his unhappiness and he worried about the tuxedo he had rented.
(pp. 152–53)

This scene too is comic, but the hurt by this time has become too
real for laughter. Cohen feels crushed and the reader must sympathize with him. His earlier awkward attempts at gallantry have
made him a ridiculous but touching figure, and now even the
absurdity of the situation cannot lessen the sense of pain. Fuchs

exposes this kind of suffering as evil not only because it hurts, but because it destroys dignity.

Realizing that "life was senseless, it had no dignity," Cohen walks to the Williamsburg Bridge, resolving again to commit suicide. This time he tries—he really jumps. In describing the jump, Fuchs provides his view of man's place in the universe:

Cohen jumped. His legs were outspread, his face covered with his arms. This was a terrible moment. In it Cohen saw reality. He became a speck in the air. His feet churned furiously, he waved his arms like a mechanical toy released. (p. 155)

Man is nothing. Certainly he is no Romantic hero magnificently shaking his fist at the heavens. Unlike Emerson's oversoul, before which "time, Space and Nature sink away,"[11] Cohen's entire being becomes a speck in the sky. Far from glorious, he becomes a pathetic mechanical toy, whose motor has just short-circuited.

As Cohen sinks into the water, he does indeed see "reality." In giving Cohen this glimpse as he sinks into the water, Fuchs is utilizing a popular Romantic notion of the sea (in Fuchs's universe the grand, rolling, titanic sea has become the East River). Here is how Fuchs describes Cohen's sinking into the East River:

He had struck the river feet first and entered smoothly. Down, down he went. His eyes were opened and he cried with fear at the black desolation of the water. (p. 156)

His perception closely resembles that of Pip in *Moby Dick*, who also witnesses the secrets of the deep. Both Pip and Cohen are saved after their experiences. Back on board the ship, Pip is unable to cope with the wisdom he has acquired: too much knowledge drives a man insane; his soul has been tampered with. He becomes a babbling child, no longer able to communicate coherently with his fellow man. Perhaps he knows too much.

Cohen is saved by a passing tugboat. He, however, does not go mad; he is merely uncomfortable. His immortal soul is strangely unaffected by the experience. Apparently modern life has so corrupted man that "soul" is no longer a viable term in Fuchs's universe. The metaphysical enigmas that torment Melville's characters have given way to lesser problems in the struggle to make a living in the

world of Williamsburg. Cohen's "sensitive" soul may be more
sensitive than most of the hardened people around him, but in the
long run he is like everyone else in his inability to attain heroic
stature. Whatever hurt Cohen's soul experiences gives way to the
needs of his body, which has the final claims on Cohen's feelings:
"Cohen meant to sit down, but the deck rushed up to hit him. The
bones in his behind hurt. He was exhausted" (p. 156).

The concept of "soul" has little validity in Williamsburg; the
primary law of Williamsburg life is, "Make a living." And the first
condition of that law is that to make a living, a good living, one must
abandon one's soul. To succeed means to engage in hypocrisy,
corruption, and theft; to be honest is to be a failure.

The most significant problem facing Philip Hayman in the novel is
to choose the kind of life he will lead: to remain loyal to his ideals and
end up like his father—honest, but poor and bitter—or to become
like his Uncle Papravel, a wealthy racketeer. Harry, Philip's brother,
has already opted for the latter choice. He often writes to Philip to
convince him to join with Papravel, who represents success in
America. Having begun as a petty racketeer, Papravel has worked his
way up to controlling an organization and a business. In the world of
free enterprise and competition anything goes, and Papravel will do
anything to succeed.

Papravel is Philip's mother's brother, so he probably grew up in a
religious home. He has become a gangster-hoodlum in order to
escape the poverty of the Williamsburg life. His basic goodness is
expressed in his generosity to his sister's family: he gives his
nephew Harry a job and is anxious to give one to Philip; he loves his
sister and gives her money. Cultivating a generous and dignified
facade is also a part of his game, however. His generosity may also be
partly explained as an act of atonement for his ill-gotten gains, for his
sister's family, Harry excepted, do not approve of his way of life.

But Papravel is no merely misguided sinner, but a professional
thug, and a ruthless man. His world is a violent one; his associates are
hardened, coarse criminals. They are, however, skilled operators,
doing their jobs neatly and precisely.

Papravel works for Rubin, the owner of the Empire Bus Lines; his
job is to eliminate Rubin's competitor, Morand, owner of the Silver
Eagle Bus Line. Both companies make most of their money transport-
ing the inhabitants of Williamsburg to the mountains during the hot
summer months. Early in the novel Papravel tries to persuade

Morand to get his business out of Williamsburg. His methods are smooth:

The six men proceeded then to strip the place bare. They worked with a methodical nonchalance, a businesslike coolness that was particularly disheartening. One of the Italians went behind the ticket counter and with one rip of his monkey wrench unhinged the ticket box. Like a confetti cascade the blue and white slips showered to the floor. . . . (p. 19)

Morand decides to fight back, and the sections of the novel which chronicle the gang war that results are full of incidents like this one.

Papravel is able to bully not only Morand but also the courts. His greatest triumph comes when, with the help of a lawyer, he is able to clear one of his thugs of a murder charge (for shooting a policeman), thus preventing his organization from getting unfavorable publicity. In winning this victory, however, he loses his nephew Harry. After the murder Harry returns home to his family. He feels that Williamsburg is a trap and that its people are cornered. He understands that it is futile to live on dreams, that reality is too strong a force. Harry still wants out, but not Papravel's way:

Philip, what jolted me was the time Gilhooly killed the cop. Then I began thinking about Morand . . . My delicate soul couldn't stand it and I quit. There's too much of the schlemiel in me. I guess I get it from the old man. (p. 279)

The monetary success of business, however, is Papravel's. He wins his war with Morand. In fact, he becomes so powerful that he even manages to remove Rubin, his former boss, from the presidency of the company. Papravel takes over, making Rubin a silent partner. The defeated Morand can only cry out against the system that has destroyed him:

Life was rotten. Business was rotten. In order to make a nickel you simply had to go out and cut the next man's throat before he cut yours. That was the only way to make money in this country. . . . (p. 353)

This too is the law of Williamsburg, cruel but true.

Through Papravel Fuchs exposes the sham that is the American dream: the opportunities that America offers can only be grabbed by the corrupt and the strong; only for them exists the possibility of gold-paved streets. The others are left with streets littered with old newspapers and watermelon rinds. The Jewish ideal of creating a heaven in this world is also destroyed. People (Jews) like Papravel have succeeded in turning America into a Hell. Papravel is a false Messiah, but only by following him can one hope to escape the bondage that is Williamsburg. For to be good and pure in heart is to remain a slave.

Papravel's world and life-style are paralleled on the streets of Williamsburg by the actions of Davey, a young boy. Violence, brutality, and gang wars are a way of life, permeating all layers of society. "Papravels" learn their business as children, by learning how to survive on the streets. In America the "Papravels" are made as well as born.

Living in the world of the streets, Davey devotes all his interest and energies to his gang. (In the 1930s children's gangs were a way of life in some sections of New York City. In Williamsburg almost every block had one. The various ethnic groups also banded together, sometimes having bloody battles with each other.) Encounters with rival gangs are planned very carefully; the confrontations are violent. If not for the lack of guns and other "adult" weapons, there would be little difference between the world of the child and that of the man. There is no real state of "innocence" in Fuchs's universe.

II *The Sainted Fool and the Revolution*

Despite the dogmatic uses that might be made of the Papravel and Davey stories, Fuchs is not a political writer. He writes about the capitalist structure because that is what exists. There is a note of protest in some of his descriptions, but it never swells into revolutionary fervor. Eventually Fuchs will come to blame men, not systems, but in this first novel, he is still sorting things out. Socialism is mentioned in this first novel but dismissed as an alternative to the democratic system. Fuchs puts the manifesto of the proletarian movement into the mouth of Cohen, and no further comment is required to dispose of this philosophy. Cohen, the dreamer, whose one great wish is to be a character in a Russian drama, dreams the dream of the revolution.

His second suicide attempt unsuccessful, Cohen is momentarily defeated, but his character is rooted in the *schlemiel,* and he has an uncanny ability to bounce back. Suddenly it occurs to him that these conclusions about life will turn him into a great philosopher, and he dreams anew. Enraptured by the vision of himself as a great, sought-after sage, Cohen decides to write the great philosophical work. Naturally he fails again—he can produce only ridiculous nonsense.

Tortured by his inability to write, he leaves his apartment and takes a subway ride:

Cohen always sought out the subways for his periods of despondency because the mechanical clatter and jangling metals gave him sustenance. Here he felt among heroic proportions and it seemed fitting to him. More, he relished the presence of the people in subways for then he felt his savage despair was at least observed. (p. 208)

This is an interesting aspect of Cohen, one which helps define his problem. Cohen feels the need to dream; placing himself outside the physical world in the world of the imagination helps give him a substance that he lacks in reality. In the real world he is alone, laughed at, and incompetent. In his dreams he becomes heroic, or at least noble. One of the problems Cohen faces (and indeed so does Fuchs the writer, as his need to examine his past indicates) is the need to define the self. Cohen's need for companions, or at least spectators, arises from his suspicion that perhaps after all he is nothing. Unknowable to himself, he strives to be located within the space and time of another's universe, and then to become known to another or others. Cohen then will exist, even if unknown to himself, because others perceive him. Like Poe's "Man of the Crowd" he requires people. He is frightened by isolation. He did, after all, discover emptiness at the bottom of the East River.

Upon leaving the subway, he is, therefore, attracted to a crowd that has gathered to hear a Socialist speaker. The speaker's words have a great effect on the crowd, and Cohen is swept up along with them, inspired with the proletarian ethic: "to lose oneself in a cause greater than oneself, to become part of some great movement" (p. 210). Now he has something new to throw himself into. And, to add to the charm of this discovery, he meets a girl. This promises to be even more important than the future of the party.

When Cohen next meets Philip, he is enthusiastic about his work with the party. He paraphrases Michael Gold's manifesto for proletarian literature (see above, p. 19):

In short, a book which has no definite moral for people, a book which does not communicate a lesson for a better way of living is dead. I am for propaganda.

What we do goes directly to the masses. . . . The idea is to reach the people directly, to teach them by concrete image and the story of the play. . . .

We're not interested in technique. We don't care a damn about craftsmanship and that kind of esthetic hooey. All we want is matter, substance, reality. (pp. 263–64)

He even goes so far as to describe a one-act play he is writing. What he describes is the typical plot of the proletarian conversion novel:[12]

It's about a man who loses his job. He begins by going through the usual hard-luck story of being thrown out of his flat, his wife leaves him, and he's all alone. He's broke. What can he do? He hits it out on the road, hitchhiking and riding the freights. I depict his experiences, the life on the rods, and the bums he meets. He goes all over, Texas, Oklahoma, Florida, and Canada. The point of the play is this: he was an ordinary wage slave until he got busted, but in his travels he gets to see things and begins to think. He reads a whole lot and thinks a whole lot. Then he joins the party in San Francisco and becomes a leader. There's a strike and in the end he gets killed. (p. 263)

In the mouth of Cohen all of this sounds ridiculous. Perhaps reduced to its bare bones, proletarian literature is ridiculous anyway, for what Cohen describes is basically all there is to it.

Philip once again tries to straighten Cohen out:

What are you yapping about Texas and Oklahoma for? What do you know about life on the rods? Do you know what a rod is? I've never seen one, and you probably haven't either. Why don't you cut the crap and get a good girl? (p. 264)

Reality is reality. Socialism can't change that. Philip is right; before the week is out Cohen will have changed his mind.

Philip is also right about what Cohen really needs most—a woman. Cohen realizes this too. One night he and Shura (the girl he met at the rally) go to a Greenwich village café. Cohen has high hopes of seducing her, and he tries to impress her with some political jargon and the plot of his play, but Shura is more interested in a café poet, Fleishenhacker, a real aesthete, whose imagistic poetry is the antithesis of the proletarian creed. Finally Shura leaves Cohen at the café, with the check, and goes off with Fleishenhacker. She is a fake, and by implication so is the movement—no movement composed of human beings can succeed. Cohen, crushed by his experience with

Shura, renounces the party, and when he reaches his apartment, alone, he can cry in despair.

Philip's father represents yet another reaction to the system. He has learned to live in it, and maintain his integrity and self-respect. But he has paid the price—poverty. In Jewish fiction the proud and dedicated householder, trying to maintain his self-respect and that of his family against enormous odds, is a heroic figure. Learning to live in this world is the great test of strength. Philip's father does assume almost heroic proportions in his son's eyes. Indeed, he is the only man of real virtue in a novel populated by petty, unattractive characters. But he is broken and weak. He has nothing but his dignity, and that will not earn him a ride on the subway. Philip, however, sees his father in purely heroic terms:

He had worked so hard and honestly, he was old and tired, his life was passing, and it seemed to Philip that in some way his father had been tricked. Further, the calm acceptance, or the resignation, at any rate, the aloof disregard of what seemed to Philip a tragedy, rendered him a noble figure. (p. 180)

This proud and good man, crushed by life and by time, has learned the lesson of Lear: "They told me I was everything. 'Tis a lie—I am not ague proof." The comparison is not an inappropriate one. Fuchs makes clear time and time again, through his characters, that in the modern world there is no longer "poetry or heroism." The stuff of tragedy is no longer in the stories of kings, princes, and conquerors, but in stories about people like Mr. Hayman.

Despite his poverty and age, Mr. Hayman refuses to sell his store to a prospective buyer for $5,000: " 'It would be a swindle,' he said and that was the end of it" (p. 174). Philip appreciates his father's integrity and admires the nobility of this refusal, concluding that "his father was thoroughly a man" (p. 174). But by conventional modern standards this is a foolish gesture. Even Mrs. Hayman calls her husband an idiot for not taking advantage of such an opportunity. Thus, ambivalently viewed, he is reminiscent of a Yiddish literary type, the wise or sainted fool whose innocence in the end triumphs over the "wisdom of the world."

One of the most famous examples of this type is I. B. Singer's "Gimpel the Fool." Gimpel believes everything, even what common sense rejects. His neighbors expose him to one torment after another, yet Gimpel stands fast, never embittered or crushed. After the death of his wife he wanders:

After many years I became old and white; I heard a great deal, many lies and falsehoods, but the longer I lived the more I understood that there were really no lies.[13]

The real world, for Gimpel, is "entirely imaginary," but "it is only once removed from the true world." Gimpel has managed to achieve his own redeemed Jerusalem. He can ignore the real world and dismiss it as an illusion. Herein lies his triumph.

Mr. Hayman does not feel Gimpel's triumph. Here again Fuchs overturns Yiddish tradition, while working within it. Mr. Hayman retains Gimpel's major characteristic, the knowledge that man's basic encounter in life is between "self-discipline and inner needs."[14] In this respect, he is triumphant, for his discipline and goodness have triumphed. He is, however, crushed and weary of the world. For him, unlike Gimpel, there is no triumph.

Mr. Hayman is baffled by America. One of the reasons for his disgust stems from the fact that "people here . . . remind me of the green, deformed, uneatable apples you find in a neglected orchard. No taste. No character." (p. 243). Of the people of New York City he says, "There is no friendship, no brotherhood, no genuine feeling, pity, or charity." This attitude echoes Sholom Aleichem's Tevye, who says, "With God I'll manage to get along. What troubles me is people, why are they so bad when they can be so good."[15]

Man in the modern world has become an animal. To be good, honest, and fine may be a heroic gesture in Philip's eyes but it has earned Mr. Hayman nothing more than "a cigarette and a window."

III *The Death of Love*

In the world Mr. Hayman describes, without friendship or charity, populated by people of "no character," it is not surprising to find that Fuchs's Williamsburg is a community that has lost its capacity to love. None of the marriages depicted in the novel is a happy one. All are characterized by nonstop fights and bickering, dissatisfaction, and infidelity.

Two kinds of love relationships are presented: the married lives of some of the older Williamsburg couples, and the younger people's early romantic experiences. If love ever existed in the lives of the older people, it has been dried up by time. Too many years in Williamsburg, too many years on earth. Probably the best explanation for this loss or death of love lies in the discovery made by a character in Humphrey Cobb's antiwar novel *Paths of Glory:* "Fear and pain are the complete neutralizers of sexuality."[16] In the old country constant persecution had subjected these older people to subhuman treatment; daily they had witnessed death and slaughter. In the new land they found filth and poverty, and their dreams of a new life were gradually crushed. Nothing had changed; there was still altogether too much pain. They "lived in a circle without significance." Too much time was spent trying to make a living; there was never time enough for love. In their condition they could never enjoy it; soon they forgot about it.

Money, indeed, forms the basis of the relationship between Old Miller and his wife, the first married couple introduced in the novel. Miller is a miser. The only pleasure he has in life is fondling and smelling his bankbooks, which he keeps hidden under planks in his floor. It is Miller who tells Philip that the one great truth in life is money: "Let them talk, let them write, that is it and the only thing." Miller's end comes as a result of money, when some men trick him into investing in fake jewelry. When he learns of the swindle, he has a stroke and eventually dies. On the day of his funeral there are no real tears. His sons argue about how to divide up his remaining $2,000. Mrs. Miller is more impressed by the crowd at the funeral than by her husband's death. She does cry and wail, however; it is expected.

The most sordid relationship in the novel is the one between Sam Linck and his wife. His marriage already a shambles, Linck is carrying on an affair with a prostitute, which gives him little pleasure but a certain degree of amusement. Sam and his family live with his mother, Mrs. Linck, the janitor of the building that Philip lives in. She is a sloppy, grotesque woman, who keeps guinea pigs in her apartment, which is filthy and always poorly lit. Once Sam left Williamsburg in search of adventure, but discovered nothing better in the world outside. Now he spends his days driving a truck, only to return to his mother's nagging and her guinea pigs at night.

To relieve this routine Sam has an affair with Marge, strictly a business relationship. Marge has no illusions about Linck; she doesn't believe that he has any feeling for her or his repeated conviction that he "will treat her fine." Linck means a roof over her head and a couple

of dollars now and then. She has had enough experience with men
and their romantic promises. In a story that is very much like
something out of *Miss Lonelyhearts*, she proves her point:

When I was up in Willimantic, making sometimes five dollars a day with
overtime, a guy told me he'd treat me something fine. He brought me to New
York on a joy ride and brought all his pals into the bed the first night. (p. 40)

When Linck's wife finds out about his affair, her own frustrations
are released in a violent confrontation with Marge. The fight between
the two women becomes a side show, an entertaining interlude for
the inhabitants of Williamsburg. Later Mrs. Linck (the mother) joins
the fight, and the three women tear at each other, bloody and
screaming. In Williamsburg, extreme frustration can only be released through violence.

This scene temporarily interrupts the affair, but Sam wants more
and resumes it again. He even goes to the trouble of sending his wife
and children to the mountains for a few weeks so that he can continue
to see Marge uninterruptedly. His wife returns home earlier than
planned, however, and breaks in on them. Another violent quarrel
results. Undaunted, however, Sam continues the affair, this time
renting another apartment for Marge. He starts coming home late
again, but his wife, finally growing resigned, no longer really cares:

She thought of the older couples in the house. They had fought on and off. If it
wasn't other women or men it was cards, liquor, relatives, or money. There
was always something. . . . There was no end. (p. 347)

IV   *Hooray for Hollywood*

The ideas of the younger people of Williamsburg about love and
romance are conditioned by the movies. While the younger generation is growing up, the film industry is beginning to boom. The youth
of Williamsburg are the first real children of the film age.

The movies are a place to dream—in the movie theaters "poetry
and heroism" can exist again. Movie people live with dignity, in
beautiful homes, amid hanging gardens and green lawns; they have
large cars and servants and plenty of money. Above all, they have
style, elegance, and class. They are beautiful. Nothing and no one in
movieland remind the audiences of Williamsburg or of themselves. It
is a world light-years apart from their own. Identifying one's self with
movie stars is another way to rise above the earth, another way of

avoiding facing oneself. Old Miller understands the lie behind romance, illusions, and the movies, and reveals it to Philip:

The rhythmic tumbling of the surf . . . was upon sober investigation no thing of beauty but an impersonal natural phenomenon, and the moon was a scientific fact. Folk moved about in the dinginess immersing themselves continuously in a sedative warm bath of ideals and dreams, but these were artificial and delusory as a soft waltz. (pp. 9–10)

Miller may realize this, but he is old and his illusions are gone. The young, however, continue to dance and to dream.

The difference between the resigned, experienced attitude of the old and the hopeful, romantic conceptions of the young is revealed by Fuchs in a neat juxtaposition, as he reveals the dreams of Davey and Mahler. Davey, a child just entering his teens, dreams of love, and the dream sequence is colored by movie-set images. For Davey, possibilities still seem very easily to be realized; after all, achieving a goal always comes easily to a movie hero:

He would have affairs with exciting ladies in organdy and smoke long cigarettes. . . . And now he dreams a lady in organdy is coming down to him, only he can't make out whether it is organdy, she is so indistinct, and her face is so wonderful he can hardly see it. . . . She plucks him to her as though they are swimming in water, and she clasps him to her bosom. Davey grows drowsy with love and from the look on her face it must be the same with her. (p. 68)

Mahler, an old man beaten down by life and experience, no longer bothered by things like love, dreams of something infinitely more delightful. For him, however, realizing his dream is hard. Life is not a movie, even in dreams:

He is lying in his dirty underwear on the dirty bed in the boiler room, but he is in Paradise also. In Mahler's vision there is a bathtub, three or four times larger than usual, Mahler sees it and he makes his way to it but there are obstructions everywhere. It is like walking up endless stairs. He walks and there is always a heavy door to be swung open or a rock to be shoved aside. He goes on until in the end there is a bathroom. There is the enormous bathtub and in it is wine. Mahler flops in and opens his mouth. His nose becomes a mouth and he drinks with it. . . . With his whole head, Mahler drinks the wine until finally the tub is empty. . . . (pp. 68–69)

The first star-struck kid introduced is Natie the Buller, the right-hand man of Davey's gang. Davey is in love with Yetta, but won't discuss his "grand passion" with his friend, because he feels that Natie is too young and wouldn't understand such things. Natie is quick to point out, however, that he too is hopelessly in love, with Marion Davies, the movie actress. More susceptible even than Davey, he has been unable to transfer the romantic feeling inspired by the film image to a real girl.

Davey conceives of his relationship with Yetta in glorious movielike terms. Sitting alone on his fire-escape (a reminder of who he actually is and where he actually is), he dreams of Yetta and sees himself as a movie hero. Then reality intrudes, as it always does in Williamsburg, for no real person is as suave as the movie star. Man, being what he is, lacks the movie hero's fluid grace:

There was a loud crash. A few women screamed. . . . Davey looked down in surprise. . . . He had kicked the gallon of wine through the fire escape. The purple mess, with scattered cherries and pieces of glass, formed a big splotch on the sidewalk. (p. 32)

The most tragic example of the death of love is the marriage experience of Tessie, a young girl who is in love with Philip. She fancies herself different from the Williamsburg crowds, a girl with a poetic soul, a kindred spirit to Philip. But Tessie is a fake. She is a very nice girl, but she lacks real imagination. Her "poetic" conceptions are derived from the movies.

Early in the novel she is in the midst of a dilemma, vacillating between Philip, whom she loves, and a corset salesman named Schlausser, who wants to marry her. The latter is "a good husband for the having," dependable and a steady provider. Tessie is torn between her practical side (a girl must get married and Schlausser is an excellent catch) and her romantic side (Philip is her true love; he appreciates fine things, unlike Schlausser, who is very common).

She gives a party as a gesture to Philip that she has decided to give up Schlausser. Philip realizes, however, that she is a wild-eyed romantic who does not really know what she feels or what she wants: "Ah, Tessie, Tessie, who studies the amorous postures of movie stars and tries them out on me, Philip thought, Tessie who even borrows the subtleties as if they meant something" (pp. 56–57). Philip, at an early age, understands people's pretensions (although occasionally he is subject to them himself) and the reality of the body and the flesh.

Philip is right about Tessie. She can put Schlausser out of her mind on the night of the party because he is not there. (He is on the road selling his wares). When he returns, however, Tessie's practical side reasserts itself. Schlausser represents "respectability, solidness, and marriage," whereas Philip doesn't even have a job, and Tessie can't wait for him forever.

Tessie marries Schlausser and almost instantly comes to regret it. She does not find love, nor can she find any corollary to her own experience in the novels she reads or in the movies. She calls Philip and bewails her fate: Schlausser is really very common, and he is rarely ever home; her marriage is empty, there is no romance. She hopes to add some dimension to her married life by having an affair with Philip, but he doesn't really believe in her wretchedness and refuses to oblige.

The most telling scene, and the one which captures the essence of Tessie's marriage (and all marriages, by implication), occurs when Tessie is preparing an elaborate welcome for Schlausser on the night he returns home from a business trip. The scene also exposes the lie behind the movies, and how they have succeeded in cheapening even the dreams that seek to ennoble the lives of real people. Tessie decides to fix up the house and arrange everything to look rich and decorous. The whole effect is to resemble the scene of a movie. The lady of the house must also look the part, and she tries to dress herself accordingly:

. . . The shawl slipped over her shoulder. That was more interesting. Like the movies. With her dark complexion and her black hair combed back smoothly, she looked like a Spanish senorita. (p. 300)

Schlausser finally returns home. Everything is set. Instead of the action appropriate to a movie set, however, Fuchs recounts a love scene between two *real* people:

Tessie put her hand on his head and ran her fingers through his hair. It felt greasy, and when she withdrew her hand two or three hairs, curled and shiny, clung to her fingers. She brushed her hand on his shirt.

Schlausser drew her to him with force and started pressing. She laughed sharply and pulled herself away. "You hurt me," she said. "You're strong."

"Look, Tessie," he said, "look here." He pointed to the pillow on his knee, but there was nothing. But when she bent forward her breasts hung loosely down and he could see the nipples clearly. Schlausser put his hand inside the neck of the pajamas and his fat fingers pressed her breasts softly, one after the other. Tessie took his hand out and arose.

"It's all right," Schlausser protested. "I'm your husband."
"So soon after dinner?" she asked. (p. 305)

When Tessie appears for the last time, she has invited Philip to take her to see a modern dance concert. She is still putting on airs, but, no longer concerned with the romantic possibilities of marriage, she compensates by filling her life with "the finer things." She now wears the masks of the cultured dilettante, the beautiful and urbane fashionable lady, and the society hostess. Tessie is a rather pathetic figure. She no longer has any real dignity, no character; her life is a sham. One can't really laugh at her, though her poses are funny, but one does "sigh." Philip doesn't laugh, either. To be aware of the falseness of illusion cannot deliver him from it, but only increases his frustration.

Early in the novel, when walking by the Auburn Social Club, where an orgiastic party is taking place, Philip reflects on the realities of love, and his thoughts seem to sum up Fuchs's own view. His own experiences and what he sees around him have convinced him that there is nothing ethereal about it; his descriptions make it sound rather base and low. Mankind is really not capable of achieving anything really beautiful, but only the kind of joy that Sam Linck finds in sex, a joy that is ugly and squalid. Love doesn't take place on silken sheets in perfumed rooms, but in Williamsburg. Like life, love develops as a cycle, one that turns and turns and yields ever-diminishing returns.

V *Escape*

Williamsburg is a place characterized by people hurrying about, engaged in various activities. There is no time to pause and reflect, only time to move. As has been shown, most of the people in Williamsburg seek various forms of escape to avoid the drudgery that is their lives. They can try, like Cohen, to escape through the imagination or through social involvement, or, like Davey and Tessie, by removing themselves from Williamsburg and relocating themselves in a movie scene.

There are other forms of escape. Harry Hayman tries to make money (he chooses Papravel), but finds that he is too closely bound to his father, that he cannot stomach the dishonesty. Eventually he will again leave his father and family, this time for Chicago, but he is permanently stamped by Williamsburg—he can never really escape.

Mahler, a cobbler, drowns himself in wine and escapes into oblivion whenever he can. Unfortunately, he too always wakes up to find himself still in Williamsburg.

Some people even move temporarily to different places, trying to escape the heat of the Williamsburg summer. The mountains and the beach become a kind of new frontier where peace or new possibilities may be sought. But this, too, is a delusion. Mrs. Linck goes to the mountains only to find that the people there are no different from the people at home. Fights and arguments constantly erupt in the run-down hotel where she stays; she herself gets into a fistfight with a Mrs. Klein and feels disgraced. The violence that Papravel begins in Williamsburg continues in the country. There is no change; the corruption continues even here.

Philip, too, goes to the country. His brother has invited him, and Philip is tempted by what he thinks the country can offer him. When he gets there, however, he feels uncomfortable; he longs to return home. Finding that the quiet and peaceful country also has its mystery and terror, Philip is troubled and a little frightened:

The road broke off from the open hay fields on either side of it and entered into a wood. The sun no longer shone on Philip's head and shoulders, and he missed its friendly warmth. The trees made odd noises in the wind. It was cool and dark. It made Philip afraid. Of what? he asked himself, but he was afraid. (p. 170)

For Philip as for the others, there really is no place to escape to. Every place has its own special terror and instills its own kinds of fears.

Of this very American dilemma Sam Bluefarb writes:

. . . The very urge to escape—after the Civil War especially, but most especially in the twentieth century—was born out of desperation and hopelessness, so that escape finally became not so much an act of hope, optimism, and Emersonian self-reliance as of hopelessness and confusion.[17]

The people of Williamsburg are confused. The need to escape is an acknowledgment of their own hopeless and futile state. There are no more territories like the one Huck Finn could head for. The Depression put an end to the hope and optimism of that earlier frontier, and the would-be fugitives from Williamsburg find their flight cut off by a crowded and stagnated world.

This dead end, this "no exit" situation, is most effectively portrayed in the life histories of Mrs. Linck's children, all of whom have made attempts to escape. Lillie, the oldest daughter, had a "smashed up nose that wrecked her features" (even her ugliness was violent). It ruined her life and made her the kind of desperate person who appeals to counselor-figures like Miss Lonelyhearts. Her fate is indeed similar to that of the pathetic girl "born without a nose" who pours out her agony in a letter to West's protagonist and asks, "Ought I commit suicide?" and signs herself "Desperate."[18] Lillie did try to commit suicide, "but had succeeded only in making a more ridiculous object of herself." Unable to die, condemned to live, she invented romance. One day she came home and told her mother that she was getting married. Mrs. Linck repeatedly asked to see Lillie's fiancé until, in the end, the lie had to be revealed. "Poor Lillie howled, her mother cursed like a witch, and the tenement laughed for a week."

Julie, the youngest of the daughters, was a very pretty girl who "found her encounters with boys a source of tantalizing enjoyment, a chance to tease them, to make manifest her charms. The boys on the block had a name for her" (p. 37). One day she disappeared and never came home again. For a long time no one knew what became of her, though "Philip's brother Harry had unexpectedly met Julie in a brothel . . . but had found it difficult to mention the news to her mother."

Mrs. Linck's third daughter, Bertha, was "the most sensible one." She was the only sister to marry properly, "but this was where she had made a mistake":

When she picked up her Bridgeport, Conn., sailor, a Christian, and he offered to marry her, she glibly waved the material considerations every housewife in the tenement never stopped mentioning. But after two months of wedded bliss she discovered her husband was a drug addict. (p. 38).

Thus life is shown to be a hoax; dreams are unmasked as false. Reality is the big cheat, and it is inescapable.

The only way out is death. This, perhaps, is the meaning of Meyer Sussman's suicide, the incident that opens the novel. It is also the reason for the suicide of Mrs. Sussman, who drowns herself and her two children at the close of the book. Following her husband's suicide, life has become too much for her—she leaves Williamsburg to join her sister's family in Montana. A new life awaits her there, but it is a life that is not very different from the one she leaves behind. There is the possibility of a new husband—her sister tells her about a

Mr. Silberstein, "a good Jew in early middle age" who wants to get married.

One day, however, Mrs. Sussman returns to Williamsburg rather mysteriously, a shattered and broken woman. Thereafter her house is never clean, her children are never washed or fed. Her experiences (both in Williamsburg and in Montana) have destroyed her; she too has seen reality, but lacks the strength to bounce back. One evening she takes her children and walks to the East River and jumps in.

Fuchs concludes the novel with a fire. Philip, Cohen, and Mahler are all drinking and having a good time. Cohen, still smarting from the newest scars reality has dealt him, is trying to find some new answer. He continues his eternal dialogue with Philip on the sensitive soul and the concepts of beauty and romance. Philip again tries to rid Cohen of his false romantic notions; Cohen again calls him a cynic and asks Mahler to arbitrate their disagreement:

". . . Mahler, don't you agree with me there are certain things that break a man's soul? Take yourself in Russia, Siberia, and China. Weren't there some things in your life that broke your soul?"

"In Russia, in Siberia, in China," the old man said slowly, "they nearly broke my back. . . . What's a soul, Cohen? Let them break my soul if this pleases them, just ask them to leave my back alone. Soul," he said, "I wouldn't give a rotten nickel for my soul." (p. 362)

Mahler's acknowledgment that there is no soul, or at least that life takes it away, destroys Cohen. It is the final blow.

Mahler, drunk with wine, falls asleep in the basement with a cigarette in his mouth. Soon the fire starts, and Mahler, too drunk to care, is burnt up. Cohen, on his way up to the roof to escape the fire, decides to go back to his room. Philip tries to stop him, but Cohen insists that he has forgotten his pajamas and must go back for them. He never comes out. When the fire is finally put out, he is found dead in a sitting position, struggling to get into his pajamas.

Irving Howe complains that Fuchs's "climax" is immature, that helpless before the fact that there is no way out, he uses a *deus ex machina* to help him end the book.[19] Howe's remark, however, ignores the thematic appropriateness of the fire device. Fuchs here is operating within a tradition: both Faulkner (*Absalom, Absalom!*) and Hawthorne (*The House of the Seven Gables*) use the destruction of a house to convey a novelistic idea. Hyatt Waggoner, commenting on this convention in connection with Faulkner and Hawthorne, writes:

Thematically, both concern a "design" to found a family (both authors use the word *design*) . . . both make a house a symbol of this design; both see the effort is doomed, partly because life cannot be "designed" this way. . . .[20]

Fuchs uses the convention to comment that the novelist, too, is doomed and will not be able to design life or adequately capture it in a novel:

How marvelously writers were able to perceive, clear-cut and with sureness, the causes and the actions of their characters. In life no man was known, even to himself, but in these novels the authors were able to explain their people logically. What wonder-makers! What liars! (p. 373)

He also makes an important observation on the concept of climax or drama in life:

In a book, Philip said, a fire could be an important event, it could be used to bind together a setting and a story, it offered a neat end. But actually there was no climax, no end. It went on. (p. 373)

Life is a dull, monotonous cycle, lived by plain and ordinary people. There is no drama here, and no real design. Philip (Fuchs) must finally declare his helplessness before life and art. At last, Philip is left looking out of a window, like his father, wondering what will become of him.

The dilemmas about life that Philip Hayman faces are reflected in Fuchs's own problems with his art. Fuchs examines Williamsburg carefully with despair and anger, but also with love. By the end, however, he has to admit his impotence in the face of his subject. The need to deal with Williamsburg, to exorcise it, and to understand, remains with Fuchs. Writing this first novel has not solved his problem, nor has it put his mind at rest. In his next novel, *Homage to Blenholt*, he faces these ghosts again in a different way.

Riding on the subway one evening, Philip and his fellow passengers experience something very unusual:

Suddenly a butterfly appeared. It was a small white one, but it caused excitement throughout the car. Everyone lowered his newspaper, couples ceased their conversations, to regard the butterfly. The conductor forgot to close the door, he was so amused by its appearance. In the meantime the butterfly flew about in crazy lines, panic-stricken by its dilemma. Philip wondered whether it would manage to get out and how long it would take. (p. 323)

Traditionally the butterfly is a symbol of beauty: Hawthorne, for instance, in "The Artist of the Beautiful," uses a butterfly as an emblem of Owen Warland's artistic ideal. The scene on the subway, a recurring image in Fuchs's work, summarizes the artist's dilemma: how to create a work of art out of the lives of people who spend a good part of their lives on the subway. It also reminds us of Cohen and Philip, butterflies in an environment that traps them, inhabitants of a world that really holds no place for them. Williamsburg is no place for butterflies.

The butterfly does manage to escape from the train:

Then, abruptly, as it had entered, the butterfly made a sharp swoop and disappeared through the window. Everyone returned to his newspaper and the thread of his conversation. There was a general feeling of relief. (pp. 323-24)

This relief, however, is not shared by Fuchs, Philip, or Cohen. Fuchs feels that he cannot create his own butterfly (work of art) out of the materials of Williamsburg. Philip is left in the subway—for him there is no convenient open window, and besides, he is human—he cannot fly. Cohen, on the other hand, tried to fly, but in escaping from the train, he fell head first onto the tracks below, and the train rolled over his body on its way to Grand Street.

CHAPTER 3

Life in a Barrel

IN *Homage to Blenholt*, Fuchs's second novel, the problems and the anguish that choked the first remain with him, but the tone, mood, and the spirit in which they are presented are vastly different. *Homage to Blenholt* is brisk, essentially comic, and fast-paced. It is fanciful and irreverent, and certainly Fuchs's most humorous novel. "If the experience of Williamsburg cannot be grasped and controlled, perhaps it can be laughed away."[1] Irving Howe, commenting on the difference between *Summer in Williamsburg* and *Homage to Blenholt*, writes:

Naturalism, with its massing of detail, somberness of voice and gloom of vision, was not really Fuchs' most congenial mode; he had turned to it in his first book because in the Thirties it seemed the most likely way of recording the pains of youth. Now, in his best novel, he would release his true gift, which was for an exuberant if slightly embittered comedy, a mocking play with daydreams. . . . The book rocks with zest and energy. . . . But if *Homage to Blenholt* is happily the work of a young man enraptured by the discovery of his mimetic powers, there is also within that young man another and much older one, Jewish to the core, who is never able to forget the essential sadness of things. And one mark of the novel's distinction is the poise with which Fuchs balances these two sides of himself, young and old, gay and weary.[2]

These "two sides" produce Fuchs's view in the novel, which must be termed tragicomic. In form *Homage to Blenholt* is a comic novel: here Fuchs concentrates on the contradiction in life between what is given and what is desired, the discrepancy between what a man has and what he strives for, what man hopes to be and what he really is.

The writer of traditional comedy supports the social ideal, seeing it as a constructive force. The writer of social comedy must, according to George Meredith, believe "that our civilization is founded in common sense (and it is the first condition of sanity to believe it)."[3]

The classic comic novel details the progress of some character who rebels against the existing order (which may or may not reflect traditional values), toward some final reconciliation with society and a reaffirmation of traditional values. Essentially comedy is destructive of false values and false appearances. It seeks to clear them away so that the reconciliation at the end may be constructive (a renewal of the good). If a society is good to begin with, its values are reaffirmed at the end. If they are corrupt, a new order arises to replace the old.

Fuchs cannot accept this traditional (eighteenth-century) vision, for he is very much a product of the twentieth century. The writer of comedy in the modern world questions the basic foundations upon which society rests. The twentieth century has revealed to man, with ever-increasing clarity, that the existence of man is at bottom inherently absurd. Wylie Sypher says that one of the most important discoveries of modern criticism is that the "comic and tragic views of life no longer exclude each other."[4] The modern sense of the comic grows out of contemporary man's feeling of confusion. This confusion, Sypher feels,

has been sadly wounded by the politics of power, bringing with it the ravage of explosion, the atrocious pain of inquisitions, the squalor of labor camps, and the efficiency of big lies. Wherever man has been able to think about his plight he has felt "the suction of the absurd." He has been forced to see himself in unheroic positions.[5]

This devaluation of man is at the center of *Homage to Blenholt* and of all of Fuchs's work. Man is really nothing, or at best a very imperfect mechanism. When ambition pushes him to try to be more than he is, he becomes laughable, ridiculous, or, in more modern terms, pathetic.

In *Summer in Williamsburg* Cohen speaks of the lives of people in Russian literature. The people he describes are quite similar to the characters of Chekhovian drama. The very term "Chekhovian drama" signified a balance between the gay and the weary, the tragic and the comic. Such a balanced vision, and the dramatic form that Chekov created to express it, stem from the perception of the incongruity between what is and what is desired. The dramatic conflict exists in the contradictions inherent in the condition of life itself, contradictions before which the individual will is powerless. The suffering of Chekhov's characters derives from the emptiness that is their lives and from their yearning for a complete transformation; "they want to reject the present and set off for some new and bright horizon."[6]

Fuchs, as in *Summer in Williamsburg*, expresses a strikingly similar dissatisfaction with the state of life in Williamsburg. The pattern of life depicted in that first novel corresponds almost exactly to the kind of life described by Chekhov's Andrei in *Three Sisters*, and there is a longing, especially in Cohen, for an escape to a "brighter horizon." In *Homage to Blenholt* Max Balkan also seeks this kind of escape. He longs for glory; the present life (Williamsburg) is not for him. In a speech to his girl friend Ruth, he echoes Andrei:

You say I ought to live like everyone else. What does that mean? It means living in a flat like this with a bathroom on top of you, going to a job all day and to the movies twice a week. It means listening to the radio all day, sleeping until twelve o'clock on Sunday, going to Coney Island if it's hot. . . . I don't want to live that way. It's dirty, sour, ugly. You're dead years before your time. Your whole life becomes a hot joke. All you do is wait for the grave. . . . There's no glory, no exhilaration—diapers! That's what it always makes me think of—diapers and the smell of vinegar!"[7]

The characters of both Fuchs and Chekhov find their desires choked by life's passing. The inexorable flow of time, the feeling that one's days are wasting away quickly, and the sense of one's imminent death make the burden of time heavier and the realization of wasted days painful.

While Fuchs (especially in the first two novels) and Chekhov concentrate on the conflict between what is given and what is desired, a conflict that is essentially comic, their works are permeated with an insistent tragic sense. One can say of *Homage to Blenholt* that it was begun as a lark and ends as a tragedy. Certainly Fuchs completely changes tone by the end of the novel, which finally becomes as oppressive as many of the scenes in *Summer in Williamsburg*. The seeds of this tragic ending are being planted throughout the novel, however, and certainly the ending does not come as a shock. Balancing the gay and the sad, the hopeful and the pessimistic throughout the book, as Chekhov does throughout his plays, Fuchs manages a complex vision that allows for the diversity of real life. *Homage to Blenholt*, like Chekhov's plays, can be considered a perfect example of Santayana's statement that "everything in life is lyric in its ideal essence, tragic in its fate, and comic in its existence." Later Fuchs will come down hard on the tragic aspects of life, ending the novel on a note of despair, but the earlier portions of the book demand a comic reading, complementing the dark vision with a Chekhovian sense of proportion.

The world of *Homage to Blenholt* is interesting also in its relation to that of the English social comedies of the eighteenth and nineteenth centuries. Fuchs was certainly aware of the conventions of that form: Cohen reads Thackeray's *Pendennis* in *Summer in Williamsburg* and Tessie also reads social novels that deal with upper-class society. In *Homage to Blenholt* Thackeray's *The Newcomes* is mentioned. *Homage to Blenholt* in fact can be read as a Williamsburg comedy of manners, though, again, not a traditional one, as his modern sensibility calls forth different responses from those to be met among the earlier comic novelists.

Fuchs's second novel doesn't have the elaborate cast of his first book. He concentrates here on one particular family, and a number of people who are close to it (one of the nonfamily characters eventually marries into the family). Naturally the high level of social sophistication in the English novels is not to be found here: no urbane dialogue, no gala balls, dances, teas, or horse-drawn carriages; the people in Fuchs's novel are low-class, poor, and entirely lacking in social polish.

However, there is an essential affinity between the social worlds of the English novels and *Homage to Blenholt* which is manifested in a peculiar similarity of characters. Like Mrs. Bennet in Jane Austen's *Pride and Prejudice*, Mrs. Balkan in *Homage to Blenholt* is a mother obsessed with marrying off her daughter. An exponent of the values of Williamsburg, she is forever encouraging Rita to be a little more forward with a potential suitor. Though in her own way lovable, she is a ridiculous character, primarily because of the vulgar and heavyhanded way in which she deals with social situations. She embarrasses and enrages her daughter; she is indecorous. Part of the problem is that her background is different from her daughter's—she is a product of the East European *shtetl*, while Rita was born and raised in America and derives her manners code from the movies. But in Williamsburg there is no time for the coy sophistication of the Hollywood heroine; the frantic, hysterical pace of life, reflected in the tempo of the scene, demands an inelegant aggressiveness. Mrs. Balkan's desire to have her daughter married is almost desperate: in a society dominated by laws of economic necessity, marriage means that the bride is no longer the responsibility of her parents; with Rita gone there will be one less mouth to feed and more space available in an overcrowded apartment.

Austen's Mrs. Bennet is, in fact, no more "elegant" in her motives or methods than Mrs. Balkan, and the parallel indicates a basic similarity between their worlds: both are economically oriented and place marriage on a plane of commercial transaction. Thus the exemplars (mothers) of both societies covet money (security) at the expense of the values of personal feeling. Alike in their perceptions of the danger their respective societies pose to the pursuit of human happiness, Austen and Fuchs, however, differ sharply in their responses to the problem. Faithful to the comic tradition of social regeneration, Austen projects a new, corrected society based on a reassertion of traditional values. Elizabeth Bennet eventually does marry, and her union with Darcy is a true marriage of affection and respect, achieved despite her society's commercialism. Thus her story conforms to the comic convention: the new marriage will serve as a basis for the renewed society of right values that will replace (at least at Pemberly) the corrupted values of Mrs. Bennet. Elizabeth and Darcy will be able to attempt the ideal society because they can leave behind the world of Mrs. Bennet—they have learned to live beyond her sphere.

This kind of renewal is not possible in Williamsburg, however, and so Fuchs's novels undercut and reverse the traditional comic resolution, essentially because Fuchs does not subscribe to the values of his society, which demands that man march in step, live within its bounds, and make a living to support a wife and children. And the mass society of the twentieth century allows no escape, no retreat to an isolated haven of higher values. Here every man must reconcile himself to the dull everyday routine of life.

In *Homage to Blenholt* Rita, too, arranges to marry for love, but she will be doomed to reenact this eternal pattern of existence. She understands this, knowing that there are givens in life that never really change. Unlike the union of Elizabeth and Darcy, her marriage to Munves will not make for a new beginning, but for a continuation, another turn in that same circle.

Max, Rita's brother, however, is the prime victim in Fuchs's dark comedy. Seeking to restore to life something like the heroism and grandeur of ancient times, he tries to live outside the rules of Williamsburg. But his ideals are misunderstood, and he is ridiculed as an eccentric fool by those around him. The women, who in Fuchs's world represent society (the reality principle), take him to task for his ideas: "It's wonderful for a fellow to have ideals and believe in them. . . . But, as a matter of fact, you have to be practical!"

Fuchs ends the novel on a tragic note, bearing out Santayana's dictum that "life is tragic in its fate." Unlike Chekhov, he cannot remain ambiguous to the end. By the end of the novel, Max, defeated, resolves to join society. Williamsburg has triumphed. In apparent faithfulness to the traditional ending of the English novel of manners, Max marries Ruth and decides to get a job, to reenter the mainstream of his society. It is here, however, that Fuchs inverts the terms of the convention. This marriage and this reconciliation are not moments of triumph, but of defeat. Such a capitulation to the patterns of society is no longer to be viewed as a noble and rational step toward human happiness, as a new chance to protect and enact a healthy ideal, but as a surrender of that most precious of modern man's possessions, the self. The old ideal does not even apply anymore; Williamsburg (society) is a tyrant that crushes the soul. When Max abandons his eccentric ways and becomes a "man," he dies a spiritual death. For he, too, is now doomed to live in a "circle without significance," a life that ends with "a cigarette and a window."

I *Tamburlaine in Williamsburg*

In *Summer in Williamsburg* Fuchs was too close to his material, so that the atmosphere of that book became finally oppressive. In this second novel, he seems to be able to detach himself from his material and to smile at his characters. Although it would be a mistake to say that Fuchs has succeeded in completely detaching himself in *Homage to Blenholt* (he is still involved), his treatment of the characters reflects a new perspective, as if he has backed up a bit to take in the comic angles of man's plight. The novel is breezy and reads very quickly, as the action seems almost speeded up.

The central character is Max Balkan, a *schlemiel*, a dreamer of dreams, and a bungler. He is another version of Cohen, though he is treated comically. Whereas Cohen's soul is always bleeding, Balkan is not a melancholy person. His continual failures only make him more determined to succeed. Certainly he has none of Cohen's suicidal tendencies.

Cohen is an intellectual who never stops brooding and thinking; he is forever complaining, holding dialogues about life and poetry, but never really doing anything. Balkan, on the other hand, is a physical being, always on the move; he creates an impression of perpetual motion. He is introduced while walking through the streets of Williamsburg. Later he runs around his apartment building trying to get his friends to go with him to Blenholt's funeral. At the funeral he is edgy, always moving and trying to become part of the crowd. He seems constantly excited and out of breath.

The connection between Cohen and Balkan is established early, when Balkan duplicates a gesture that Cohen made in *Summer in Williamsburg:*

. . . On Rodney Street the candy store was opening for business, the man removing the huge glass windows.
"Good morning!" cried Balkan with joy.
"Hah?"
"I'll be your first customer," smiled Balkan, nothing fazed. "Lemon-lime please." (p. 13)

Balkan is presented here as a man of zestful energy and a certain aggressive sociability, a direct contrast to Cohen in a similar scene:

. . . The Italian ditch-diggers on Metropolitan Avenue resting on the sidewalks after the day's work looked up at this strange Jew walking defiantly in his private cloud of gloom. Cohen stopped at a candy stand. He pointed to an inverted bottle of lemon-lime.
"You want five-cent drink?" the man inside the store asked. Cohen pointed to the jar again and gestured that he could not hear or talk, reluctant to waste conversation on the man. (pp. 207–208)

Balkan is like Cohen, however, in his desire to escape Williamsburg. He is a dreamer, constantly scheming and inventing get-rich-quick ideas that will enable him to get away from an environment that degrades him. Max walks in the early morning, dreaming privately, picturing himself as heroic, living with glory:

At seven o'clock the streets of Williamsburg were barely awake, there was no humiliation, no indignity, and it was possible for him to feel a man, living in great times, with grandeur and significance. (pp. 12–13)

Obsessed with this idea of reaching for power and glory, Max dreams of chains of hot chicken-soup stands, plans for announcing movie programs over the telephone, piping in music on the subway, and bottling onion juice. Unaware of the comic incongruities of such Williamsburg heroism, he aspires thus to recreate a world reminiscent of the "glory that was Greece, the grandeur that was Rome." His ideal hero is Tamburlaine, and he longs for that ancient conqueror's power. He realizes, however, that in modern-day America the acquisition of empire must be accomplished by different methods:

In a way I am Tamburlaine, only in Williamsburg, now, not a shepherd in the olden days. I can't win out by conquering kings the way he did. I've got to get ahead by making money. That's the difference, but behind it it's all the same thing. (p. 75)

A Tamburlaine in Williamsburg! From Ripple Street to Olympus! Max longs to live with majesty and dignity amid the sound of cymbals and the blowing of trumpets.

The main action of the novel involves Max's plan to attend the funeral of Blenholt. He feels the need to pay homage to this man, who, according to Max, did manage to rise above the common and gain distinction. Blenholt seems to him the modern Tamburlaine, but what Blenholt really is is another story. When Ruth asks about him, Max replies, "Oh, a hero . . . I told you, Commissioner of Sewers" (p. 80). The use of the term "hero" is significant, for it says a great deal about the modern age and what passes for a hero in America in the 1930s. Before Max can really answer Ruth, his sister Rita tells the truth about Blenholt: "Blenholt was a diabetic, Ruth. . . . Don't listen to a word he says, he's nuts as usual." The tragic flaw of today's hero is a weakness for sugar. Max is angered at this intrusion and defends Blenholt:

A hero in this flat age! . . . A racketeer, a gangster, a grafter, a politician, anything you want to say, but a hero! Like an emperor in the olden days! Tamburlaine in 1935! Blenholt was a hero! (p. 80)

But Blenholt is no hero. He certainly exhibits none of the qualities of heroism as described by Carlyle in his *On Heroes and Hero Worship,* which Max cites in one of his hysterical panegyrics on Blenholt. In truth Blenholt was a criminal whose "power" was based in graft, manipulation, and theft. Fuchs's ultimate comment on his "flat age" is this elevation of Blenholt. In an age that has no room for ideals, heroes must conform to debased standards, for there are none in the chivalric mold. If the twentieth century were to add a seventh chapter to Carlyle's book, it would be "the hero as racketeer."

The truth about Blenholt is revealed to Max at the funeral, which

forms the novel's centerpiece, one of Fuchs's finest sustained pieces
of writing (Irving Howe calls it "immortal"). Max has spent a good
part of his time during the first part of the novel trying to get his
friends Coblenz and Munves to attend the funeral with him. When
they fail him, Max drags Ruth with him, under duress. Ruth feels that
Max is crazy and, besides, "Joan Crawford's at the Miramar" and she
would rather be at the movies, worshiping her own brand of heroism.

The funeral begins rather well. There is a "flamboyant funeral
march" played by "seventy flutes and brasses." It is solemn and
dignified, with the grandeur of a great state occasion, and Max is
overwhelmed: "What a funeral! . . . What a procession! This is what I
mean when I say that reality doesn't have to be dingy. This is heroic!"
(p. 155).

Like everything in Balkan's life (as in the life of any of Fuchs's
characters), however, the funeral fails to live up to its glorious
beginnings and Max's expectations. A woman in a Buick sedan who is
in a hurry to get somewhere tries to drive her car across the path of
the funeral cortege. Taken aback by this, Blenholt's men tell her to
wait, but she refuses. Max decides to be heroic and intervenes
("Balkan, proud, hoped that Ruth would take notice of his achievement"), whereupon he is insulted by the woman and by Blenholt's
thugs and then loses sight of Ruth. "In another minute he was
swallowed up in the crowd until he stood outside on the fringe" (p.
157).

This last image is significant as a foreshadowing of Max's future. In
the beginning of the novel he is shown as enveloped in a cloud of
unreality, dreaming, isolated. When he becomes part of the crowd,
he symbolically becomes a part of reality. For Max is really only
human, an everyday person, like the people who make up the crowd.
His failures at heroism and his momentary disappearance into the
crowd reveal the eventual loss of the sense of uniqueness and identity
that he will suffer. This brush with reality does not teach Max his
lesson, but other incidents will.

Blenholt's men dispose of the problem created by the woman by
slashing her tires. Like Papravel's men, they are professionals, doing
their work quickly and methodically. The description of Blenholt's
men at work is very similar to that used to describe the operations of
Papravel's crew, and the repetition of this type of character and this
type of scene emphasizes the importance of the gangster in American
life.

Max, shaken but still undaunted, finds Ruth and proceeds to the hall to hear the eulogies and the funeral services. The services are secular, for while Blenholt spoke Yiddish at synagogues and Italian at church weddings, death has revealed that he was neither Jewish nor Catholic but, in the opinion of some of his followers, "some kind of Turk."

The services are banal and dull. Fuchs parodies stylized, impersonal eulogies delivered at funerals. The speeches are too long and the audience become restless. They soon regain their spirits, however, when an old woman faints and disrupts one of the speeches. Soon things degenerate completely. First a Williamsburg businessman, disgusted by the splendid picture of Blenholt that is being painted by the speakers, stands up and attempts to expose Blenholt for what he really was:

Good money we made with sweat and blood we had to give out of our own pockets. Give, he said and the bums with the pistols in their hands said give, and we gave like it was a hold-up, we gave! We gave until we got pushed out of business altogether. (p. 164)

The man speaks in vain, for as he is carried kicking and screaming from the hall by Blenholt's men, the audience calls him a Communist and decides that he was sent by the Communists to cause trouble. The "agitator" disposed of, the services continue, but not for long. The woman victimized earlier by Blenholt's gang disrupts the service, demanding payment for her tires. She mounts the speakers' platform and begins beating the speaker. Blenholt's thugs descend on her, the crowd comes to life, and bedlam erupts. Max, pained by the whole affair, again decides to be heroic, and again he is shown up for what he really is—he is violently trampled by the crowd.

In a scene which predates West's great crowd scene in *The Day of the Locust*, Fuchs vividly paints a picture of a man caught in the midst of an uncontrollable mob:

Max tripped and fell, his spectacles dropping from his ears to the floor. In a sudden lurch the circle about the raging woman took it into its head to swerve over Balkan. Three or four men stumbled heavily over him. . . . People kept digging their heels into all parts of his back, kept falling down on him with force every time he tried to raise himself to stand up, they smashed his face into the wooden planks until the skin was rubbed away and little dots of blood appeared. The breath was squeezed out of him. He couldn't get up. The stampede punished him as he choked for air. Balkan felt as miserable as a man ever felt. The angry swirl went on like a nightmare. (pp. 168–69)

Swallowed up by the crowd again, Max learns about the reality of people like Blenholt, and the real truth that lies behind his illusions, this time in a very painful and violent way. Fuchs's description of a man hopelessly caught up and trapped in the midst of mob violence is indeed similar to West's and might be an influence (*Homage to Blenholt* was published three years before *The Day of the Locust*). In both cases the writers depict mobs who have been cheated. Fuchs's people have been victimized by men like Blenholt, who under the guise of benevolence have in reality robbed them. West's people have also been cheated, stripped of their illusions, and they are bored, defeated, and broken down. In West's final scene they are stirred to destruction by the emptiness of their existence, the same emptiness that Max will soon have to face.

Max emerges from this scene bloody, nauseous, and without his glasses. He is also alone, for Ruth, disgusted by his behavior, has already left him. He must make his way back to Ripple Street, a somewhat disillusioned man. Weak, bruised, a bloody mess, and feeling defeated, he walks the littered sidewalks that he now very much resembles, toward home.

II   *The Company of the Meek*

Max's friend Munves is also a *luftmensch* and a dreamer who seeks to avoid Williamsburg by trying to live outside of it or ignoring it. Munves is an etymologist and linguist whose greatest joy lies in finding errors in scholarly footnotes; he spends all of his time holed up in his room tackling minor linguistic problems. His intellectual ability notwithstanding, "most of the housewives on the landing said that he didn't know enough to wipe his nose without being told."

Munves has promised Max that he will go to the funeral with him, but when the time comes, Max can't get him to respond or to get ready. The scholar is in a world all his own, a world that has little room or time for Blenholts or funerals. Max has no patience with Munves or his linguistic problems and he considers Munves a "nut," which is ironic, for it again is a reflection on Max's ability to perceive: he is able to see through the essential unreality of Munves's world but not of his own. Munves, on the other hand, can sympathize with and under-stand Max's conceptions of heroism. He is able to recognize a kindred spirit in Max, for he experiences the same scorn from a community that sees little value in his work.

Despite this kinship Max has little patience with his friend and calls him "hopeless." As Max leaves him to get ready for the funeral, Munves happens upon another scholarly mistake, and, preoccupied with this problem, he forgets about the funeral.

Munves is in love with Max's sister Rita. She also loves Munves, but neither of them will talk of such things to the other. Proposing is the male's prerogative, and Munves, unfortunately, is an innocent. In matters pertaining to sex (or anything worldly) he remains a child, despite Rita's best efforts to get him to commit himself or make an advance. In Fuchs's novels, especially this one, the women are this-world oriented, while the men are dreamers. Women know that dreams do not put food on the table, that to eat, one must have money, and to get money one must have a job. Rita's primary task, however, is to get a husband, and she knows how to play the game. She decides to woo Munves by taking an interest in his work. She is really the only one with whom Munves can share his enthusiasm for linguistics, and he delights in telling her all about his latest discoveries.

Mendel Munves, linguist, like all of Fuchs's characters, has a touch of the dreamer in him too. His announcement of a new linguistic find is accompanied by a brief reverie in which he pictures himself "the man of importance, the man of action" (p. 134). This dream, like all dreams of glory in the world of Williamsburg, results in a pratfall. Again the dreamer is brought down to earth:

Munves began a sigh but at that moment he lost his balance, on the chair which rested on only two legs. For ten seconds he groped in the air madly, tried to grip the underside of the table with his knees, opened his mouth to gasp with the fear of crashing to the floor. But Rita was quick and straightened him out. The chair banged on all four legs again. (p. 135)

The language here is significant. Munves indeed lives on air, and Rita will eventually "straighten him out." Like the chair, Munves will in the future be forced to place both feet on the ground.

Rita, though rooted in reality, also dreams. She understands the world that she lives in, but a longing to escape from it is a natural reaction. She dreams of a singing career, but this magic spell, too, is shattered by an intrusion of reality. Munves has a callus and wants Rita to take a look at it—this is Rita's real career.

As Rita examines his hand, suddenly and for the first time, Munves becomes excited by her presence. His remark, "Do you know, Rita, you smell like a calf" (p. 137), signals an awakening physical response.

His reaction to the girl is reminiscent of Benjy in Faulkner's *The Sound and the Fury*. Benjy, the idiot boy, associates his sister Caddy with trees, and repeatedly says, "Caddy smells like trees." Munves's experience with girls (reality) is as limited as an idiot boy's and the implied association with Faulkner is deliberate on Fuchs's part.

Munves also has sexual fantasies. Frequently he daydreams of caressing Rita in a bathtub of warm water. He asks her to teach him how to dance, and as their bodies touch Munves begins to talk of love. His statements, however, remain abstract and general; finally he asks Rita to be his "companion." Rita is excited but perplexed. "Had Munves actually been making love to her all this time?" She replies:

Companionship . . . is a wonderful thing. You don't have to tell me. . . . Companionship is why people get married and I think that is the cornerstone of every successful marriage. (p. 142)

The mention of the word "marriage" frightens Munves—this is the real thing. It involves more than taking baths together. He becomes frightened and confused as he contemplates the consequences: it certainly would mean an end to his own private world.

Munves, a shaken and frightened man, returns to his studies. It is hard for him, however, to ignore Rita's flesh as she bends beside him, and fantasy soothes his fears:

To be married! Actually to take baths with Rita! These things were possible. To sleep with Rita in the same bed every night, their naked bodies lying side by side! If some one could give Munves a guarantee that Rita would sleep without pajamas, he felt he could almost reconcile himself to the prospect of marriage, terrible as that was. (p. 149)

With thoughts of baths and soft flesh hovering over him, Munves turns his mind, once again, to linguistic research.

As in *Summer in Williamsburg*, children play an important part in this novel. Heshy, a young boy, unlike Davey of the earlier novel, is not a rough-and-tough child of the streets, but meek, one who is afraid of playing on the streets and would rather stay in the house with his mother. The main cause of this fear is Chink, a bully who is continually teasing him and pushing him around. Heshy lacks the courage and strength to fight back and prefers to avoid the embarrassment that would result from a confrontation.

Max identifies with Heshy: "He was one of his, a compatriot in the army of the meek" (p. 197). Both are temperamentally unsuited to the harshness of Williamsburg life. Heshy is more comfortable playing with little Goldie, even though he doesn't like the idea of "playing with girls." Like Max, he would like to think of himself as something more than he actually is.

In one sequence Fuchs employs the cinematic device of cross-cutting in depicting parallel scenes between Max and Ruth and Heshy and Goldie. During the scene Max is trying to convince Ruth to go with him to the funeral, while Ruth, as usual, is telling him that he is crazy and ought to get a job. Their argument is cut into occasionally by a scene showing Heshy and Goldie playing a game. These separate scenes finally coalesce and dissolve into each other.

Confusion develops into slapstick as the two scenes converge. Heshy, running away from Goldie, runs into Max:

"Go to hell and drop dead," Hesh cried, victorious, for he had managed to bang past Balkan's hips out of Goldie's reach. Max was knocked down the steps. He tried to secure his glasses as he fell and at the same time Goldie struggled sticky-fingered over him. (p. 35)

The scene ends with Max sprawled foolishly on the floor, and Heshy, still afraid that Goldie will hurt him, hiding behind a nearby staircase. Goldie (like all the women in the novel) has the last word. It is a very funny scene, but tinged with sadness. The strong seem to get stronger and the meek just continue to lose.

III *The Underground Man*

Coblenz, Max's other friend, who is also supposed to join him at the funeral, is the most problematic character in Fuchs's fiction. The scant critical analysis the novel has received has tended to place Coblenz in the same category as Balkan and Munves, a *luftmensch* and a dreamer whose problem seems also to lie in a limited perception of life. This is not really accurate however; Coblenz is quite different from his two friends. A major problem in the understanding of Coblenz is that he is the only major character in any of Fuchs's novels who succeeds: he places a bet on a longshot horse and the horse wins. Dreams never come true in Fuchs's novels, and the fact that such a boon is granted to one of his characters raises large questions: Why does he win? And what does his victory represent?

Coblenz is labeled by Irving Howe "a naive cynic who is completely at the mercy of his sensations."[8] This is not completely true: he is a cynic, but far from naive. And rather than being at the mercy of his sensations, he consciously controls them. Coblenz has his roots in Dostoevsky's Underground Man. Fuchs has taken Dostoevsky's character, pared him down, and placed him in Williamsburg.

When Coblenz first appears, he is trying to cure a toothache by drowning himself in liquor, which is only making things worse, heightening the pain:

Leave it alone, I say to myself, but I can't, I got to make it worse and then I am drinking cold water over it to numb the tooth. . . . Then all the teeth on the side begin to hurt until I figure, it's no use kidding, I got a toothache. . . . So I get the whiskey and the more I drink the worse it gets. (pp. 21–22)

The Underground Man opens his narrative by complaining about his liver:

I am a sick man . . . I am a spiteful man. I think my liver is diseased. . . . I refuse to treat it out of spite. You probably will not understand that. Well, but I understand it.[9]

Both Coblenz and the Underground Man are in pain and both refuse to do anything about it. The Underground Man "understands" his motives and it is the purpose of his narrative to make them clear to the reader. Coblenz also "understands." He acts as he does on purpose.

The Underground Man refuses to accept any kind of law or formula. He is against science, the laws of reason, and man's whole systematic accumulation of knowledge. To indulge his own will is what he desires:

You see, gentlemen, reason, gentlemen, is an excellent thing, there is no disputing that, but reason is only reason and can only satisfy man's rational faculty, while will is a manifestation of all life, that is of all human life including reason as well as all impulses.[10]

It is for this same reason that Coblenz has little use for theories. When Max tries to suggest something that may alleviate the pain in his tooth, Coblenz becomes suspect. "Is this a theory?" he asks. When Max assures him that it isn't, Coblenz agrees to listen. Unfortunately what Max suggests *is* a theory and Coblenz will have no more of it.

If theories exist to delimit experience, then Coblenz's freedom will be hindered by any application of theory. This cannot be and he will not allow Max to shackle him with such "nonsense." The words of the Underground Man help explain Coblenz's attitude:

> I believe in that freedom, I vouch for it, because, after all, the whole work of man seems really to consist in nothing but proving to himself continually that he is a man and not an organ stop. It may be at the cost of his skin! But he has proved it; he may become a caveman, but he will have proved it. [11]

Coblenz, like the Underground Man, becomes an example of unrestricted freedom. Dostoevsky's character, according to Edward Wasiolek, is a man whose "free, foolish, unfettered caprice is his only weapon against the laws of nature, and his only gauge of freedom. He can know his freedom only by acting his freedom. Consequently, he must dramatize to others, but most of all to himself, that he is free." [12]

Coblenz, too, is defiant and spiteful. If the children upstairs want to bother him with their noisy skating, he can get back at them. He inserts a pin in the doorbell of their apartment, causing it to ring continually, which drives the mother of the children to distraction. Coblenz laughs joyously (and spitefully) over his victory. When Max comes to Coblenz's apartment to ask him to get ready for the funeral, he decides to threaten him and frighten him away. Later he does the same to Munves, actually attacking him with a knife.

Such irrational behavior is calculated and spiteful. His threats are spoken in a tone "of complete normalcy." It is a performance, and Coblenz enjoys giving it. This wild and unrestrained caprice is a weapon, the measure of his freedom. He must show others and himself that he is free. If these people consider themselves friends of Coblenz, and want to help him, then Coblenz will overturn these conceptions, threaten and intimidate them. He has no need for anyone, and can redefine his relationships with people anytime he pleases. None of the people in the novel really understands him, however, and he is pitied and dismissed as "nuts."

Coblenz believes in nothing except his will and his freedom. He holds nothing sacred and is extremely cynical. At times he indulges in moments of reflection; like Cohen, he dreams of producing "a great work of literature that would immediately shame the whole race into wholesale self-slaughter"—the title of this work would be "Epitaphs and Epitaphs."

Coblenz is a bundle of contradictions (a Dostoevskian sign of freedom). He despises his fellow man ("Ninety-Nine out of a Hundred People Are Lice"), yet has a deep-seated affection for Mrs.

Wohl, the janitor (he gives her a box of candy), Balkan, and Munves. He can tease Mrs. Wohl and associate with a tough crowd and yet have compassion for Munves when his cronies pick on him ("Lay off, you lousy bitches, why the hell don't you have a heart"). He leads an irresponsible life (he doesn't work and hangs around bookies) but longs for responsibility ("My folks, . . . they were good jewish working people").

Coblenz loves to bet on the horse races and always has hopes of making a big killing at the track. His one dream during the novel is related to this:

Zambina, Queen of the Zambesi, fair and like unto a willow tree, is sprawled out on her belly at his feet. . . . Suddenly a cloud of dust is spied in the distance. It is Karatchka The Curt, dashing madly on his pure blooded white stallion. A wave of the hand. The music stops. The daisies stop. Zambina rises. Down from the saddle swings Karatchka. He kisses the ground before his master.

"Sire," he pants, "Latabelle won the fifth race at Empire City and she paid twelve to one."

"It is nothing," drawls Sherif Coblenz. . . . A wave of the hand and the music, the daisies, Zambina continue. (pp. 106–107)

The fantasy is interesting, if ridiculous, and it assumes a certain significance when placed beside the Underground Man's own opinion of dreams:

. . . I had a means of escape that reconciled everything—that was to find refuge in "the sublime and the beautiful," in dreams. Of course I was a terrible dreamer. . . . Dreams were particularly sweet and vivid after a little vice. . . . There were moments of such positive intoxication, of such happiness, that there was not the faintest trace of irony within me, on my honor. I had faith, hope, love . . . I should come out into the light of day, almost riding a white horse and crowned with a laurel. I could not conceive of a secondary role for myself, and for that reason I quite contentedly played the lowest one in reality.[13]

Coblenz, too, plays a "low" role in reality, though his escape takes a rather less noble form. His dream demonstrates again how the modern age has debased ideas of heroism and beauty. The whole sequence is colored by cheap movie-set images: chorus girls and zebras amid the daisies and the music. The use of horses is important: all thoroughbreds (race horses) are derived from the blood of three stallions, all Arabian. In the spirit of the Arabian Nights those champions were prized for their beauty and speed; horse races were epic contests, inspired by the love of competition. In the modern age the horse is valued only for how much it will win at the track. "Karatchka the Curt" now spurs on his "pure blooded white stallion" in order to speed the news that Latabelle "paid twelve to one"; the economic spirit has replaced the Olympic. And Coblenz confirms the validity of this comment on modern values by waving off the message, for Coblenz is the eternal rebel against his society's ways. Finally rewarded in the economic terms so dear to the heart of Williamsburg, he dismisses its messenger and turns disdainfully back to his plastic dream world. His vision of Zambina is pure escapism, like the Underground Man's white horse and crown of laurel; when a nearer reality intrudes, with its conventional formula for happiness, he rejects it immediately in favor of the remoter illusion.

Max Balkan's dreams are fulfillments of his waking desires: believing in possibilities, theories, and success formulas, he actively seeks the heroic stature that fantasy here confers on him. Coblenz, on the other hand, loudly scorns such conventional aims, and his dream represents a rebellion against even the irresponsible, unearned kind of success he does aspire to in life. In his dreams Max "escapes" by succeeding where he fails in life, while Coblenz projects in his fantasy a wholly unreal situation, beyond the reach of society's confining systems. Max lives in dreams; Coblenz dreams to escape from life.

And again unlike Max's, Coblenz's dream does not last, for, like the Underground Man, ". . . the period of my dissipation would end and I always felt terribly sick afterward. It was followed by remorse. . . ."[14] After his drunkenness and his dream, Coblenz, too, returns to the struggle with reality, and it is then that he decides to write "Epitaphs and Epitaphs" to reassert his rebellious nihilism. Like Dostoevsky's hero-antagonist, he knows that such dreams are merely "intoxication," delusion. Like an "appetizing sauce," they add a certain flavor to existence, but beyond that they are false and of no value.

Coblenz, because of his philosophy and way of life, stands outside of the Williamsburg society that he lives in. He is a man apart, ridiculed, laughed at, and pitied by his neighbors; his desire for freedom and self-definition forces him into this position. Max, as indicated, is somewhat outside of the community also. His desires and aims, however, while grand, are socially acceptable. The achievement of the rags-to-riches dream is, after all, the American dream; one can't really fault Max for trying to achieve it. Munves's scholarly pursuits are also socially acceptable. Coblenz's life-style, however, is completely alien to Williamsburg. He recognizes this himself: "This kind of life was wrong for him—goyish—boozing, betting on horses, hanging around with driftwood. . ." (p. 113). He continues, however, to gamble and drink. This too is necessary for to work would be to fit himself into a pattern, and he can't do that. By denying his essential "Jewish" self, he asserts his freedom to define himself in his own way.

IV *Charlie Chaplin in Williamsburg*

Mr. Balkan, Max's father, is another figure whose roots reach back to the first novel. He is closely related to Mr. Hayman, though, like many of the characters in *Homage to Blenholt,* he is treated comically. Both fathers are passive, wise, and weary. Fuchs's first comment on Mr. Balkan's character links him with Mr. Hayman: "As for Mr. Balkan's desires, he has reached the point where he didn't want anything. And, the sad truth was, nobody asked him in the first place" (p. 58). Mr. Balkan's air of resignation relates him to Mr. Hayman, but the second line of this comment points up the difference between the two. While Mr. Hayman is a respected figure, endowed by both Philip and Fuchs with a kind of nobility, it is immediately apparent here that Mr. Balkan commands little or no respect from the members of his family. Fuchs elaborates, sketching Mr. Balkan as a clown:

He was dressed in a resplendent patched checker suit, and his shoes, easily ten sizes too large for him, were not only bulbous but lacquered red. Between them and the cuffs of his trousers, flaming socks showed. In keeping with the enormous size of his shoes and suit, the collar around his neck served merely as an ornament for no giant would have found it small enough. His face was smeared with white powder, apostrophes of white paint punctuating the area about his eyes below the two black circumflexes which were drawn above them. A great big red-painted nose like a baloney sausage. (pp. 58–59)

The costume of the clown makes him a laughable figure, but the implications of his appearance are serious. In a very modern sense, he can be viewed as a Beckettian figure who, in Jan Kott's words, "assumes a clownish attitude towards fate."[15] Such an attitude is revealed in the complete indifference with which Mr. Balkan views things.

He came to America full of hope, full of life and desire. He became an actor with the Yiddish theatre, traveling all over the world with Yudensky's troupe. As an actor he played the great classical roles, "nothing but the best": Hamlet, Macbeth, Othello, King Lear, and Tamburlaine. People, however, had little money for the theatre in those days, and Yudensky could not pay his actors. Mrs. Balkan opened a grocery store, but this, too, provided little money. Mr. Balkan was soon playing bit parts on the Bowery, and then there was no work at all. Now he dresses up as a clown and carries a sandwich sign that advertises Madame Clara's Scientific Beauty Treatments. He is laughed at by his wife; "Mr. Fumfotch" she calls him. The most he can do is recall the "great days" when he was a successful actor. He recalls Macbeth's "Tomorrow" speech, thereby confirming his own notions about the absurd and empty quality of life, "a tale told by an idiot, full of sound and fury signifying nothing."

Life no longer really bothers Mr. Balkan, nor does the constant nagging and teasing by his wife. All he asks is a little quiet. The years have taught him "that in this world pleasure was often only the denial of pain." He lives by recalling his yesterdays, and by burying himself in his *Tag* and reading the *Bintel Brieve*. Here there is peace and that is all he asks.

In several ways Mr. Balkan is closely related to Charlie Chaplin's Tramp character, as Mrs. Balkan suggests: "It was bad enough when he was young but in his old age he's a real Charlie Chaplin." The novel even begins on a Chaplinesque note. Max's own walk is reminiscent of Chaplin:

His gait was a peculiar one, involving a delaying, circular movement of the right hip which had the effect of kicking his right foot sharply forward in order to maintain the necessary rhythm. The repeated recurrences of that hip movement with its ensuing foot kick resembled spiritually, at least, the constant snifflings of a nose-cold sufferer. (p. 11)[16]

Max is Chaplinesque, too, in his defiance of convention and in that everything he tries results in a pratfall. His ambitions, however, differentiate him from the Tramp, who is not a seeker of power and glory. Mr. Balkan, too, has resigned any aspirations, and he is the real Chaplin figure here.

Like the Tramp character, Mr. Balkan is a figure who endures. He possesses the ability to go on, even to dance. Every day he puts on the sidewalk sign and walks the pavement sidewalks of the city. He never really complains, for he has learned to live in the world. All he asks is

to be left alone, so that he can live out his remaining days in peace.
Like Chaplin's tramp in the film *Modern Times*, Mr. Balkan dreams of
freedom, peace, and the outdoors, and the parallel between the two
becomes certain when Fuchs writes:

Mr. Balkan was a Charlie Chaplin, a fumfotch, he begged for quiet and read
the Tag, he craved to float in the still waters of continuous passivity. That was
because his wry wisdom had instructed him long ago that in this world
pleasure was often only the denial of pain. To close one's eyes and ears, to
bury oneself behind a paper, to overlook telephone bells, to hide in toilets
from excitement that was comfort and happiness, and that alone. (p. 209)

Chaplin's Tramp is, above all, a moral figure. Robert Payne writes
that "he came to birth in an age when morality was in decline" and
that "he could come to birth only in such an age."[17] He appreciates
human-dignity. Here it is helpful to recall Fuchs's contention that
this is a "flat age," dominated by people like Papravel and Blenholt.
The true heroes, people like Mr. Hayman, who can manage dignity,
are left with nothing. Mr. Balkan, too, is an honest and moral figure.
Despite the absurd appearance he presents in his clown costume, he
is lovable, admirable, and oddly heroic. Above all he is a moral figure,
and in the end he assumes a position of dignity and wisdom.

On the day that Max comes home from the funeral, crushed
because he is beginning to learn that people like him have no real
place in this world, Mr. Balkan tells him a story which explains Mr.
Balkan's essential goodness as well as the reasons why he doesn't
really fit in in the modern world. Max (who is very much like his
father) is meant to see himself in the story:

Max, when I was a boy in Kiev, in the old country, there was a dog, such a
funny dog. The craziest dog you ever did see— all mixed up, you know. One
part of this, another part and another and some more parts all mixed up. But
one part was from a hunting dog somewhere and he knew it was given him he
should hunt. So when he went into the fields, the first thing he would look for
the animals in the bushes. He could smell them or something, but he could
always find them and he knew it was asked from him he should get the animal.
But he couldn't get it because the hunting dog in him, it wasn't strong enough
or something. So he would yip and yip and cry like an angry baby, he would
raise an awful holler, because after he smelled out the animal he could never
get it. (pp. 209–10)

Mr. Balkan does not have it in him to be a "hunting dog," or a
Blenholt. He is a good man and because of this he must content

himself with a life that leads to "a cigarette and a window," the fate of Mr. Hayman. This specific connection is made later in the novel when Max, getting up in the morning, "saw his father sitting at the window. . . , the yellow sun on his face emphasizing his years and his weariness. Mr. Balkan looked only old and weak and tired" (p. 229).

Mr. Balkan recognizes that honest work is futile. He tried acting but failed and now he is back at work. It is honest, not exactly pressing in a shop, but it too is futile. Yet of all Fuchs's characters none is really more loveable than poor Label Balkan. The reason for this lies in his peculiar dignity, that same clownish nobility that makes millions of people love Charlie Chaplin. It is Fuchs's achievement, like Chaplin's, that he is able to elevate such a clown to a position of nobility and to make him a figure whom all readers must respect. Max, in looking to Blenholt for inspiration, is looking in the wrong place. He is too young to notice his own father, with whom he shares a room. Here is a real man, in a world that has no room or desire for this vanishing breed.

V *Victories and Defeats*

The various denouements of the novel come quickly, and in the end the fates of the various characters merge as all is resolved.

Balkan comes home from the funeral physically beaten: his glasses have been broken, his nose is bleeding, and he feels nauseous and weak:

Farewell to glory. There was something about physical violence, something about a punch in the nose bringing blood, that routed immediately all ideals and speculations. Before a punch or a kick, philosophy became unreal. (p. 181)

Ruth, in the meantime, has returned to the Balkan apartment without Max, which causes a real uproar as the family begins to worry that something terrible has happened to Max. Ruth and Rita commiserate with each other, for both are in love with men who are dreamers. Their lot is a difficult one, but they will endure, for they are strong; they embody the life principle.

Max's arrival on Ripple Street triggers a great deal of excitement. The family is all over him in seconds, Mrs. Balkan becoming hysterical. Max, sick from his latest failure, wants to hide.

Munves, meanwhile, rushes into the room in a state of great

excitement. He has made a "great" discovery, and doesn't notice that
no one really seems to care. He doesn't even see that Max has been
injured, and begins to explain his "find" to him. Then he is
interrupted by Coblenz, who rushes into the apartment and begins
running around the room. Coblenz, the Underground Man, is in
constant motion; no one will catch him. Having exhausted all
possibilities of his own milieu, apparently he seeks to find "in motion
what has been lost in space."

While Coblenz is running maniacally around the room and Munves
is busy trying to interest everyone in his discovery, Max contemplates his own situation. The lessons of reality are painful, and
they do not come easily:

My ideas are right and that's what makes it so hopeless. It's because I know
what I want to do and because I can't. Don't you see Ruth, I don't want to be
like everyone else. It's dingy, dirty, small and uncomfortable. . . . I want
more. I want to live grandly, to have a nice home, cars, servants, power,
money. And I want to live with a little majesty and dignity. . . . When I walk
the streets I want people to say: "That's Balkan." . . . The way they did when
Blenholt was alive. (pp. 204–205)

Ruth patiently tells Max that life doesn't work out the way he thinks it
should. She can't explain it; that's merely "how it is." There really is
nothing wrong with Max except that he is human. His lot must be like
that of millions of others.

Blenholt is really no hero. Fuchs moves away from the tenement
for a moment and focuses on Blenholt's men, "hired cutthroats who
had made him what he had been." They are all boors, ignorant men
who find their minds preoccupied by other matters now that the
funeral is over: they discuss the Brooklyn Dodgers, the horseraces,
and how foolish their boss was to eat so much candy. The men
conclude their discussion by agreeing that Blenholt was really "an
all-right guy."

Max's grief, however, doesn't last very long. He receives a
telephone call from Mr. Atwater of the Onaganda Onion Company,
thanking him for a letter he has sent them (Max has suggested that
they bottle their onion juice and recommended the slogan, "No
peels, no odor, no tears"), and asking if Max can come to see him at his
office the next day. Max is ecstatic: now his dreams will come true; he
has finally made it. He crows to Ruth, "I'll be rich, richer than
Blenholt!" (p. 224). Amid all this excitement, Rita and Munves come

in to announce their engagement, but the effect is lost on everyone except Mrs. Balkan.

The next morning is a time of triumph for Max, as he basks in his new image as a tycoon. His mother and sister treat him with respect and he is full of grand ideas. Mrs. Balkan begins to tell everyone in the building of Max's great success. Only Mr. Balkan is troubled, feeling that it is too early for congratulations, that nothing substantial has really happened yet.

This sense of excitement is balanced by Munves's sense of foreboding about his engagement. He is now thinking of opening a delicatessen store, though in his imagination, it will be more of a literary salon:

I have a theory about delicatessen stores. In the old days the wits of the time gathered at coffee houses and inns. Will's, the Mermaid Inn, and so on. We haven't places like that today, and I often think of a delicatessen store with tables in the back where people can drink tea, eat meat sandwiches and exchange the gossip of the day. (pp. 241–42)

Munves's thoughts again are rather sublime, but Mrs. Balkan brings him down to earth by misinterpreting his whole concept:

In Williamsburg . . . all the young ladies, they don't cook like the older generation. Lunch they eat in the delicatessen stores with the baby carriages outside, and in the night when the husbands come home from work, they throw together pastrami, cole slaw, potato salad and finished, supper. A delicatessen store these days is a fortune. Good, Mendel, you're a smart boy, a delicatessen store. (p. 242)

Everything is measured in terms of dollars and cents; people no longer have any use for places like the Mermaid Inn. Life in the modern world consists of quick lunches, quick getaways, and the movies.

While Max's new fame spreads and Munves frets over marriage, Coblenz is having a bad day with the horses. He has been losing all day and needs a break, which is finally provided by Munves, who is taking a walk in the area where Coblenz and his friends hang out. Deciding that he must "broaden his vision," Munves has decided to explore the places populated by tough-guy types and drunks. Coblenz's friends recognize him and tease him, calling him "Mr. Pishteppel." Coblenz rescues him from these people and then asks his advice on picking a horse. Flattered by the attention, Munves begins to read aloud the names of the horses running in the next race, one of which is called Lativich. When Coblenz hears this he goes wild: here is Latabelle, his lucky horse! He sells his coat and bets everything he has. Lativich, he later finds out, is an old horse, one that hasn't raced in years, a real longshot. Coblenz's buddies laugh at him, but Coblenz is sure, and he is right. The horse wins and Coblenz collects $300.

Coblenz is not the only one granted a victory in the novel. Heshy, one of the meek, also tastes the fruits of success. With the help of Goldie, he manages to lure his arch-enemy Chink into a dumbwaiter and trap him there. Momentarily allowing Chink to open the dumbwaiter door, he bombards him with rotten grapefruit rinds filled with ketchup and garbage. The brainy Heshy has finally triumphed over the strong but stupid Chink, and Max, who comes upon Heshy during this proud moment, shares in his triumph:

Hesh was one of his, a compatriot in the army of the meek, his victory was Max's also. There it was, Max said to himself, power, the meek arisen for once among the proud. (p. 197)

Early in the novel a character is introduced who makes a few brief appearances and then is never heard from again, an aged pearl peddler who goes from apartment to apartment trying to sell his wares. He intrudes on Max twice when he visits Munves and Coblenz, on both occasions knocking on the door and interrupting Max's conversations with his friends. Max, like Coblenz, has little patience with the peddler, an emissary from the world of reality (Williamsburg). He is irritated because he cannot define for himself the significance of the peddler's intrusion, or perhaps because he subconsciously does recognize him and refuses to acknowledge what the man represents. The old peddler is a kind of "Ancient Mariner" figure, one whose presence and haunting cry for money will instruct the dreamers in the lessons of reality. His lesson is something that all men must learn, and Max and Munves will learn it by the end of the novel.

Max's hopes for fortune and success are, as usual, castles in the air; his meeting with the president of the onion company is a disaster. He is informed that the company has been bottling onion juice for years; and the president gives him a three-pound bag of onions in gratitude for his interest. Max walks home with his eyes closed. Unlike the mood that animated him at the beginning of the novel, he is now

capable of feeling only pain: "it cried only for forgetting, for anes-
thesia, in the same way that a soldier tortured by his wounds demands
urgently morphine."

This defeat changes Max. He bids farewell to his youth and his
dreams, and accepts reality:

> There was nothing for him to do but to surrender, to go to work, to pay his
> debt to his father, to Ruth, to the world. . . . Forget Blenholt and Tambur-
> laine, be like the millions of others! How long a fool, tortured with visions
> among the clouds? How long a dreamer? Reality hit him in the face until he
> knew he should have realized years ago that his struggle was hopeless. (p.
> 293)

Max goes to Ruth and proposes marriage, the agency of defeat: "He
felt cold now, with no trace of tears for himself. That was all over.
Balkan felt himself a man" (p. 293). Max and Munves are now tied to
marriage, and must face the prospect of getting jobs and making a
living.

The final gesture, however, belongs to Coblenz. Sensing the air of
defeat that pervades the Balkan apartment, he nods in recognition of
Max's stupidity. Coblenz has understood the futility of Max's quest all
the time. He also notices the bag of onions, the symbol of Max's
failure, and thinks to himself, "The poor little dope." He then
jokingly and cynically suggests to Max that he convert to communism:

> Max ought to have a revelation . . . and turn Communist. A great cause
> uplifts the spirit when it droops. . . . It's a new happy ending. You feel lousy?
> Fine. Have a revelation and onward to the revolution. That's heroism for you
> and you can feel you're elevating to the stature of man not only yourself but all
> of mankind. Anyhow, it's a great feeling at a time like this. (pp. 296–98)

Once again Fuchs comments on the validity of the proletarian
movement, this time through Coblenz, the Underground Man, who
knows that no cause will free man. Communism is a trap, like every
other system. Coblenz will have nothing to do with causes. Through
him, a more perceptive judge than Cohen, Fuchs can again mock
those who feel that political solutions will solve man's problems and
alleviate his pain.

Everyone is beginning to get annoyed with Coblenz and they ask
him to leave. Unperturbed, he sees his friends poised on the
threshold of reality and decides to make one final grand gesture.
Fuchs's description is significant:

Coblenz had been absorbing all the punishment without saying a word, without moving a muscle. Now he rose slowly. He couldn't resist it. It was like being God and the impulse was too strong for him to disobey. (p. 298)

He gives Mrs. Balkan the $300 he has won. Like Dostoevsky's Underground Man, who also discovers the effectiveness of exercising his will over other wills, Coblenz's desire to control the situation is another sign of his struggle for freedom. Ironically, however, his gift will permanently destroy the freedom of Max and Munves, who will use the money as a down payment on a delicatessen store. Coblenz's gift will tie them to the kind of life that leads to "a cigarette and a window." Coblenz himself soon experiences pangs of regret. It is the typical reaction of the Underground Man, illogical and contradictory:

Three hundred dollars. It was true the impulse had been irresistible, but why had he given it all away? He might have kept something for himself. (p. 299)

Heshy's victory over Chink is also shown to be tainted. Having won his victory, Heshy proposes an alliance with the enemy. In doing this he turns on Goldie, his only friend and the one who helped him gain his only triumph. Irving Howe writes:

Even if the meek triumph momentarily, they must forego the purity of motive that had sustained their meekness. In the very act of triumph their meekness sours into pride, and their tenderness into arrogance. [18]

Everyone is happy over Coblenz's unexpected generosity. Ruth suggests they celebrate by going to the movies; Joan Crawford is still playing at the Miramar. This outlet alone remains for dreams; it is the only escape permitted from Williamsburg.

The last words belong to Mr. Balkan, the foolish Mr. Fumfotch. He must get ready once again to strap the boards of his sandwich sign to his shoulders and walk the city streets. Everyone has left and for once he has peace and quiet. Alone he can indulge his fancy in dreams of success and respect. But even his imagined dignity is shortlived: his wife interrupts the reverie, laughing at him and again calling him "Mr. Fumfotch." Mr. Balkan can only ask for quiet and leave. His final thoughts end the novel with a death knell and a fitting epitaph. In his thoughts lies Fuchs's theme:

In his wife's earthly guffaws he recognized the clamorous demands of the world, its insistent calls for resignation and surrender, and he knew now that

Max would never be the same again. Much had gone out of Max, aspiration, hope, life. His son would grow old and ageing, die, but actually Max was dead already for now he would live for bread alone. That was the rule and few men were strong enough to disobey it. It had happened to Mr. Balkan himself, he knew, and now it happened to his son. And regretting the way of the world, Mr. Balkan realized that he had witnessed the exact point at which his son had changed from youth to resigned age. Walking out of the house and shifting the shoulder straps to get the signs comfortably settled, it seemed to the old man that this death of youth was among the greatest tragedies in experience and that all the tears in America were not enough to bewail it. (p. 302)

The modern age with its way of life has killed the spirit. In a debased world, the heroes are people like Blenholt and the good man becomes a clown, an object of laughter.

What began as a lark ends on a note of sadness and resignation. A man may laugh or try to daydream his way out of Williamsburg, but in the end he must strap a weight to his shoulders and walk the streets. Mr. Balkan will now be joined by his son and his son-in-law. They, too, will now step to the music and march, and the procession will grow and the line will stretch on. Man indeed bows out with a "whimper."

When Max, bloody and defeated, comes home from the funeral, the members of his family descend upon him anxiously and hysterically. Everyone is concerned and the normal routine of the day is upset. Into the midst of this mayhem comes Coblenz, who begins to run madly around the apartment. This prompts Munves to observe:

"Like an hysterical butterfly in a subway train. . . ."
"Like a what?" Rita asked him in honest curiosity.
"Like a butterfly," Munves explained. "He ran out of the room like a butterfly that came into a subway train by mistake and finally flew out. . . ." (p. 201)

Munves compares Coblenz to the butterfly, but the analogy can also be extended to Max. Max, like the "butterflies" of the first novel, wants to escape what Williamsburg represents. He wants to restore to life (mostly to his own) the concepts of "soul" and grandeur, terms that no longer have any meaning. Max, of course, never escapes the subway—by accepting "reality" he becomes a passenger, doomed to ride the train until he dies.

Munves's comparison of Coblenz to a butterfly is also apt, though Coblenz is a very different kind of butterfly. In a sense, like the butterfly, he escapes the subway, though he manages it by never really getting on. He doggedly pursues his ethic of freedom, which allows for no ties whatever, spiritual or manmade. He doesn't let himself get trapped. He retains his freedom by great effort, and yet, ironically, it is apparent finally that Coblenz is really no happier or better off than any other character in Fuchs's world.

In Dostoevsky's universe the Underground Man is not really a positive character, for his freedom manifests itself in a destructive will. The freedom is bought at the price of a kind of terror which results from this freedom. In Dostoevsky the solution to this problem is God, but Fuchs's characters can find no God, and no way out. Coblenz can only face the "horror" his freedom exposes him to—he is basically a miserable man.

In *Crime and Punishment* Dostoevsky turns the Underground Man into Raskolnikov and has this young student test the implications of freedom. The ultimate act of freedom becomes murder. Raskolnikov kills and is imprisoned, but is saved when he finds God. In his next novel, Fuchs will present an extension of Coblenz. He too murders. . . . Perhaps it is better, after all, to just ride the train.

CHAPTER 4

"Children of the Cold Sun"

WHEN Fuchs sat down to write *Low Company*, the last novel he was to publish for thirty-four years, the kinds of conflicts that had plagued him in the earlier novels had disappeared. Gone are the wide-eyed dreamers and searchers like Philip, Cohen, and Max Balkan. Fuchs is no longer searching for solutions; the last novel is a portrait of a world on the verge of collapse, a vast wasteland where everyone and everything is *dreck*. Irving Howe, writing in the 1940s about Fuchs's career, noted the tone of surrender:

In his first two novels he had tried to develop themes and construct images that might carry his work beyond himself and to the shores of some general meaning; but in his last novel he acknowledged skillfully and sadly, that his quest for meaning was at an end. He had searched but had not found. . . .[1]

Low Company is Fuchs's finest novel, technically his most surely plotted work. All of the major characters are in a sense grotesques, but they are also immediately believable. It is Fuchs's distinctive achievement that he can keep his characters so real and lifelike, even while he bends and misshapes them to convey his message. Here Fuchs surpasses Nathanael West, who could paint nightmarish landscapes as well as anyone, and populated his world with figures who fit perfectly within the context of that world. West's characters are basically realistic, but they are not for the most part three-dimensional, being rather exaggerations of symptoms than total personalities. Fuchs's characters, while also grotesques, might be found in any neighborhood.

The comic sense that permeates *Homage to Blenholt* is absent from *Low Company*. The comedy in *Homage to Blenholt* is good-humored: Max's longings are understandable, for the desire to be more than he is and also the failure to do so are common to all men. Max is an innocent; he is very likable and his quest is a noble one. Like the clown, he wants to go on dancing and dreaming to the end, and his audience wants to dance with him.

Low Company offers few humorous passages, because here Fuchs is describing a sick society. It is hard to laugh, but, to borrow West's phrase, very "easy to sigh," for Fuchs is dealing with the "truly monstrous." In this novel it is more difficult to identify with the characters (though Fuchs certainly believes that all people possess some of the characteristics he is describing) and easy to feel superior to them. One laughs uneasily at their baseness.

The humor is not, however, as one critic describes it, "sardonic," nor is the book "savage."[2] Fuchs must have written the novel in a state of great despair, but not in a spirit of hatred or even excessive anger. Harold Strauss, reviewing the book for the *New York Times*, finds that, in Fuchs's hands, "harsh . . . and noxious realism . . . can be deeply tinged with beauty. Fuchs has been empowered to work this miracle by the great charity in his heart."[3] Fuchs's contemporary James T. Farrell recognizes this aspect of Fuchs's writing:

Sympathy is a dominant note in Fuchs's writing. He has a keen eye, an excellent ear for the speech of his characters, a quick perception of the grotesque, the whimsical, the pathetic, the tragic in modern crowded urban life. And underlying these capacities is a genuine respect for his characters, for the human animal. No matter how repulsive his characters may be . . . he portrays them with sympathy.[4]

Farrell and Strauss are right: the novel is dominated by a sense of sympathy and even of forgiveness. If this is Fuchs's most damning study of life, it still retains the compassion of his earlier novels.

Low Company should be read as a dramatized world view. Most of the action takes place at Ann's, a soda parlor at Neptune Beach (Fuchs's equivalent of Coney Island or Brighton Beach). The protagonists are all of the same low social rank, and the action of the novel takes place within about forty-eight hours, during which time the lives of the characters become inexorably intertwined and their destinies are worked out. The novel is a vision of a world running down; each episode and character reveals the spiritual decay of modern society.

Low Company can, in fact, be read as a prose "Waste Land." The novel does not attempt a prose transcription of the poem, but it does portray essentially the same kind of world that Eliot depicted in his poem.[5] *Low Company* is preoccupied with ugliness, decay, violence, and the disappearance of the human. In short, the world is presented here as a vast wasteland, "a dead land," a "cactus land."

Eliot's "unreal city" becomes, in Fuchs's novel, Neptune Beach. It is to places like Neptune Beach that the people of Williamsburg long to escape in *Summer in Williamsburg*. Here supposedly is a place where people can enjoy themselves: there are beaches, water, fresh air, space, and the ocean breeze to take the edge off the summer's heat. Neptune Beach, however, offers no escape; it is no better than Williamsburg, perhaps worse. One goes there hoping to find fulfillment, but instead finds nothing. Like West's California, Neptune Beach seems a promised land but is in reality a desert.

Fuchs's description of Neptune Beach reveals it for what it is, "unreal," a place without foundation or substance. It is a slum, a modern garbage heap:

The sidewalks were broken in all those places where the blocks caved in. . . . Everything in Neptune Beach was sand. It was a misery. No matter how hard the street cleaners worked, shoveling the sand in mounds along the gutters, more blew in from the beach. On rainy days you walked in black gritty mud. Nothing was solid, neither the pavements nor the foundations of the buildings.[6]

The residents of the area frequent places like Ann's, an over-decorated ice-cream parlor, featuring loud colors and futuristic designs. Here one can feel enveloped in unreality:

Dividing the parlor into two sections ran a five-foot wall, also Chromo Art-Metal, topped every yard by a great electrical fixture of red, green and yellow panes, matching the walls. And at the very end of the store, behind a gleaming show window which was lit at night by three one hundred-and-fifty-watt bulbs and in the daytime by a specially constructed skylight built in the roof just above it, was the ice-cream machine, Mr. Spitzbergen's pride, his greatest after his wife. (p. 4)

It is the characters, however, who provide Fuchs's focus in the novel. The human element is ultimately the force that shapes Neptune Beach and makes it what it is. Fuchs opens the novel with an epigraph from a prayer said on Yom Kippur, the Jewish Day of Atonement. It sums up the reasons for Fuchs's despair and reveals why society must ask forgiveness:

We have trespassed, we have been faithless, we have robbed, we have

spoken basely, we have committed iniquity, we have wrought unrighteous-
ness, we have been presumptuous, we have done violence, we have forged
lies, we have counselled evil, we have spoken falsely, we have scoffed, we
have revolted, we have blasphemed, . . . we have done wickedly, we have
corrupted ourselves, we have committed abomination, we have gone astray,
and we have led astray. O, Lord our God, forgive us for the sin we have
committed in the hardening of the heart.

The key phrase here is "hardening of the heart," for this is the
primary cause of most of the evils enumerated in the opening of the
prayer. Indeed, it is the basis of Fuchs's greatest despair.

Cleanth Brooks, in writing about "The Waste Land," states that the
degeneration of man, in Eliot's view, is one of the primary causes of
the modern wasteland:

The fact that men have lost the knowledge of good and evil, keeps them from
being alive, and is the justification for viewing the modern waste land as a
realm in which the inhabitants do not even exist.[7]

Fuchs's "hardened men" (they are not quite hollow) do not quite fit
this description, though they are not far from it. In certain ways they
are even worse. Fuchs's people know what good is, but find that it is
easier to do evil. Occasionally they may be bothered by conscience,
but it is merely a passing annoyance, for soon they harden themselves
anew. It is every man for himself, no one has time to think of his
neighbor, nor is there room for kindness or consideration. Man has
lost that unique capacity to be "human." In the modern world (or
Neptune Beach) all have become "low company."

The company to be found at Ann's is a "low" group indeed. All the
workers and the loungers there are locked up within themselves,
trapped by their inadequacies and temperaments and victimized by a
society that encourages their dreams but delivers nothing. Like West
in *The Day of the Locust*, Fuchs provides a crowd of silhouetted
figures—the cheated, the wounded, the nameless many—as a
background against which the actions of the main characters take on
their full significance. These foreground figures are the fully embodied
portraits of modern disintegration.

I   *"For the Rain It Raineth . . ."*

Mr. Spitzbergen, the owner of Ann's, is, in financial terms, a
success, and thus a rarity in Fuchs's fiction. (He is really the first

major character who is a successful businessman, since Rubin, the owner of the Empire Bus Co. in *Summer in Williamsburg*, is a minor character who does not figure prominently in the action of the novel.) Unfortunately, money is Spitzbergen's whole life. He gets no pleasure from it, yet he dies a thousand deaths every time he has to pay a bill. His obsession with money distorts him and eventually kills him. If not having money traps one in places like Williamsburg, Spitzbergen proves that having it creates other traps that are just as horrible, and dangerous as well.

This novel, like *Summer in Williamsburg*, opens with a rainstorm. In the first novel the rain was considered a welcome break from a hectic Williamsburg day; the people were able to go indoors, the street merchants closed up, and there was a brief time of quiet. It was also a relief from the heat, cooling the air and the hot pavement. In this last of the Williamsburg novels, however, the rain and bad weather are seen as a curse, at least by Spitzbergen. (It is interesting to note that in Fuchs's wasteland it is always raining, while the hoped-for rain in Eliot's poem does not come until the end.) Spitzbergen curses the climate because bad weather means poor business. The hot weather brings the people from the city to the beach, but when it rains, the people stay home. No one is around to eat Spitzbergen's breakfast specials or dig into one of his famous ice-cream sundaes.

The weather, indeed, is an actual dramatic factor in the novel. For Spitzbergen it almost becomes a character, one even more sinister and dangerous than the mob organization that threatens him. He feels that the weather is deliberately turning sour just to harass him and destroy his business.

The weather is not Spitzbergen's only problem. There is always something to complain about, such as his beautiful wife, who is draining him financially by her hypochondria and constant trips to the hospital for check-ups and tests. The only time in the novel that Spitzbergen experiences any pleasure is when she comes into the store, which is named for her. He is proud of her beauty and enjoys seeing her, but this comfort is only temporary. The money she costs him is always gnawing at him, and the demands of the outside world overshadow even those of his wife. Making money is his primary law; before this, family and love must take a back seat. In this, Spitzbergen is a less sympathetic figure than the older family men in the earlier novels, Mr. Balkan and Mr. Hayman, for whom business took a back seat. Spitzbergen significantly has no children, but has invested his life in his business instead. He is "one of the deformed, uneatable apples . . . you find in a neglected orchard" that Mr. Hayman refers to in *Summer in Williamsburg*. In the universe of *Low Company* men like Mr. Hayman have ceased to exist.

As if the demands of his wife and the unpredictable weather were not enough, Spitzbergen finds that he is involved with a mafialike organization. He has considerable property-holdings in Neptune Beach, among them apartment buildings which he rents to a man named Shubunka, who uses them as houses of prostitution. Now a mob is in the process of gaining complete control over the houses of prostitution in Neptune Beach, slowly eliminating all of the small-time operators. During the course of the novel they concentrate on Shubunka and, though him, Spitzbergen. Thugs representing the boss order Spitzbergen to get rid of Shubunka, and to show him that they mean business they smash up his ice-cream machine.

The mob in this novel, while similar to both Papravel's and Blenholt's in certain respects, differs from them in one particular that is significant of the change in Fuchs's vision in this novel. This mob is a nameless force. The head of the organization is never seen, nor is his name ever mentioned. The hired cutthroats also have no names, only nicknames. Anonymity increases the terror, and this mob is more disturbing than those in either of the previous novels. In *Low Company* the mob is pure evil, delighting in destruction and murder. Fuchs is now intent on displaying the world's ugliness for what it is, occasionally even rubbing the reader's face in the mud of Neptune Beach and letting him smell it.

Spitzbergen doesn't know how to deal with the mob. Underhanded dealings make him nervous and he does not really know how to react. He feels that perhaps he should get out of the land business altogether, for if he gets involved with the mob they will suck him dry. He pities Shubunka, but there are more important considerations—"the two weeks' rent money he owed him." For fear of losing money, Spitzbergen promises the mob that he will drop Shubunka and then turn him in. His concern about betraying Shubunka does not stem from a desire to save a fellow human being's life (though he thinks of this occasionally), but from his fear of losing the rent money.

In a rather pathetic scene later in the novel, Shubunka, at the end of his rope, promises Spitzbergen that no matter what happens to him the rent will somehow be paid: "Don't worry, Mr. Spitzbergen. You'll get the rent. Somebody will bring it to you whether I'm in this world or not" (p. 214). Spitzbergen, completely unfeeling, can only react with, "Who? . . . Who will bring it to me?" Shubunka can drop dead as long as he is all paid up.

In keeping with the novel's "Waste Land" motif, Spitzbergen can be seen as a kind of debased fertility-god figure. He is at the center of the novel; all of the characters revolve around him. He is the employer of most of the major characters, and Karty, who is not employed by him, practically lives in his store, and Ann's, his soda parlor, is the center for much of the action of the novel. The name, Spitzbergen, is German for the "top or peak of the mountain," which is fitting, since Spitzbergen is indeed the top man in the economic hierarchy of the novel. Considering him a god figure is also in keeping with Fuchs's theory (developed over the course of the three novels, and hammered home here) that money has become the one reigning god in America. Spitzbergen represents the money ethic in its most grotesque form. Interestingly, it is his death at the end of the novel that seemingly puts an end to the bad weather: on the morning after he is murdered the sun comes out, the people hurry to the beach, and business once again prospers in Neptune Beach. The wasteland revives once the god has been sacrificed.

II *The Innocent and the Tough Guy*

Shorty and Arthur are two employees of Ann's who figure prominently in the action of the novel. Both are types, but they are drawn with a sureness that animates their personalities.

Shorty is a marvelous portrait of the pseudo–tough guy. A soda jerker who has notions of being a suave ladies' man, in complete control of all situations, he could easily have come from the Chicago streets of Studs Lonigan. Shorty is a fake, his whole personality a sham. He is the real "hollow man" of the novel, for he has lost claim to his own identity and in its place has manufactured a web of substitute roles which seem to him superior to what he really is.

He is also a debased version of the dreamers of the earlier novels, Cohen and Max Balkan, who understand the poverty of their existence and try to overcome it. Their victories can be achieved only in the imagination, for they are human and forever tied to Williamsburg. Each tries, in his own way, to reconcile his own life to his particular dream world: Cohen's final response to Williamsburg is to escape it through suicide, while Max decides to accept it and live in it. Ultimately, however, they both abandon their poses and accept what they are. Shorty, on the other hand, has no real understanding, and lacks the sensitive, artistic temperament of the earlier protagonists. His tragedy is that he has come to believe in his pose and allowed the "dream" personality to replace the real one.

More than just a depiction of unethical and corrupt business practices, *Low Company* is a portrait of a world stricken with a great poverty (as its epigraph implies). In this regard it seems to have been influenced by the writing of James T. Farrell, especially his masterpiece, the *Studs Lonigan* trilogy.[8] Farrell, when planning the Studs Lonigan novels, was aware, according to Edgar Branch, of the way economics and a slum environment affect human life. Farrell, however, decided to go deeper and display the effect of "spiritual poverty on character."[9]

Shorty is a classic case of a bankrupt society's influence on the content of character. Subscribing wholly to the values and ideals of his social environment, he has destroyed his inner self in the rush to imitate the celluloid heroes of Williamsburg. As has been pointed out, the movies provide the main outlet for escape in Fuchs's Williamsburg; they are also a major cultural force, a force that retards and stifles the spiritual growth of the individual.

The movies are in Fuchs's world, as in Farrell's, a cultivator of images. In Shorty's case, and the case of Studs Lonigan, the image implanted is that of the tough guy. The violence which pervades the novels that tell their stories is a sign of the cultural ideal that animates such products of the film age. In one sequence Studs Lonigan is watching a movie *(Doomed Victory)* about the rise and fall of a gangster, Joey Gallagher, with whom he immediately identifies. What Studs admires in Gallagher is his tough stance, his ability to handle "dames," and his violent attitude toward life, "afraid of no goddamn thing in this man's world, giving cold lead as his answer to every rat who stepped in his way."[10]

Shorty, too, admires this image. Physically anything but the tough guy, he is always trying to compensate for his physical inadequacies. One evening on a date to the movies, he yells at a man behind him who has asked him to keep quiet during the film. After he calms down he reflects:

He had shown Madame Pavlovna what sort of guy he was. Looks were deceiving. Sometimes the strongest, toughest, gamest men were the smallest. Small size, big heart. What the hell, said Shorty to himself. He dropped his arm as if absently on the corsetière's heavy thigh. (p. 220)

Life is reduced to a pose. People are seen as labels, not as individuals, and love is reduced to sex.

Shorty is involved in the only real comic sequences in the novel. More than anything he yearns for a date with Madame Pavlovna, the corsetière. She comes into Ann's every morning for breakfast, and Shorty always gives her extra-special service and consideration. The Madame is a somewhat affected woman, always reminiscing about her past, when she traveled around the world and was very rich. Shorty thinks her the classiest woman he has ever met (she is also well endowed), an excellent companion for one as worldly, mannered, and sophisticated as the soda jerker considers himself. One morning when she is speaking longingly of the past, Shorty decides to ask her for a date; when she has accepted, "he felt like Ronald Colman and exhaled grandly." Later, when he dreams about his upcoming date, the dream is colored not by romance or love but by the hope of sexual conquest. The effect of the dream (like all dreams in Fuchs) is broken by the intrusion of reality. A messenger from Madame Pavlovna comes to tell Shorty that the corsetière won't be able to make it. " 'A stand-up!' shrieked Shorty. . . . That was what it was, a stand-up. The soda jerker had steamed himself up all day and now he was in a frenzy with frustration."

The next day, smarting from the wounds of rejection, Shorty is cooler to her, no longer rushing to serve her breakfast and speaking brusquely to her. Madame Pavlovna is hurt by Shorty's behavior and sends him a note, thus beginning a very amusing exchange of letters. The style and spelling of these notes again show the lie beneath the pose, for the correspondents are simple, uneducated people whose pretensions cannot hold up in any real situation. Shorty's letter exposes the shallowness behind his airs:

Dear Mrs. Pavllovna:

A freind in name is no freind in deed. As the provurbe is. I thought you are my freind I was wrong about it. Live and lirn that is my mottoe. While I thought you are my freind you were appairantly just having your flinge with me to you I was just the soda jerker at Anns. Well we all make mistakes all the time I made mine about you.

Yours truly,
The Soda Jerker

The letter-writing produces results: Shorty finally gets his date.

Arthur, who works with Shorty behind the counter, is the most
innocent of Fuchs's characters. His personality is childlike, and in
essence he is a child, with no real place in the adult world. His
innocence makes him very vulnerable, and, as a result, the lessons he
learns and the education he receives take on a dimension of terror.

Arthur's closest literary relationships are with Wing Biddlebaum in
Sherwood Anderson's *Winesburg, Ohio* and Homer Simpson in
Nathanael West's *The Day of the Locust*. Fuchs probably read
Anderson's book and was influenced by it, as was West. *Low
Company* predates the publication of *The Day of the Locust* by two
years, and West may have been influenced by Fuchs, for Arthur's
story in many ways resembles Homer Simpson's.

"Hands," which is the first story in *Winesburg, Ohio,* deals, as do
all the other stories in the book, with human isolation. Wing
Biddlebaum's hands symbolize the gap in communication that exists
between him and the community. They are a plea for help, but they
isolate him and make him a grotesque. Man's estrangement from his
fellow man is also a dominant theme of *Low Company*, though Fuchs
deals with it in a different way. When Arthur is first introduced, the
link with *Winesburg, Ohio* is established immediately:

Arthur ran hot water into the second basin and started to clear the counter of
the cups and dishes which he piled neatly, deriving artistic pleasure from the
job. Especially it fascinated him to drop the crockery into the water. How
softly the dish sank to the bottom when he placed it flat on the surface. What a
gentle swirl as the water covered the plate. And what nice bubbles from the
soap flakes. Arthur's hands lingered dreamily in the hot water as he placed
the dishes one by one into the basin. (p. 11)

Arthur lives in a world of his own. He seems barely affected by
Neptune Beach, or what goes on around him. Shorty considers him a
"crazy mutt" and says that Arthur is "asleep on his feet." This is an apt
description, for Arthur lives in a semiconscious state (like Homer
Simpson), more at home in his dream world than in the real one. He
aspires to be "free as a bird with nothing on my mind, with enough
money in my pocket to get along on and a little something extra
besides." The achievement of this state is, of course, impossible, for
no one is free in Fuchs's universe, but Arthur prefers to keep himself
in a state of reverie and think about it.

Arthur, like Shorty, is a victim of his culture's debased ideals. He
has an almost childlike adoration for what he considers to be worldly

or tough in others, for he is totally lacking in these qualities himself. He enjoys going to the movies:

. . . his mind was then lulled to a sort of sleep so that for two hours in the darkness the vacant monotony of uninteresting life became suspended and he lived adventurously with the actions of the hero and heroine on screen. (p. 224)

It is this yearning that links Arthur most closely with the lost tribe of *Winesburg, Ohio*, of whom Randall Reid states: "They are alien from their surroundings, yearning for a lost past or a promised future which will end their exile and fulfill their dreams.[11] This is the kind of world that Elizabeth Willard dreams about for her son, that West's grotesques come to California to find, that Fuchs's people seek in Neptune Beach, and that Arthur finds in the movies. Arthur, like West's Homer Simpson, is a representative and embodiment of the vast crowds of empty people who flock to California and to Neptune Beach, people who lead empty lives and yearn for excitement. Arthur *is* the nameless crowd of the cheated "primitives who have suddenly inherited decadence. The dull yearning of their lives has, under a steady diet of lynchings, murders, sex crimes, become focused upon phantoms of excitement, phantoms which have no real home."[12]

III   *The Damnation of Coblenz*

The ethic of the Underground Man pursued by Coblenz in *Homage to Blenholt* is explored by Fuchs again in the character of Moe Karty, who does indeed live underground, having abandoned his wife and adopted the basement of Ann's as his new home. Like Coblenz, Karty is a gambler. His entire day is spent in studying the race-track forms in the newspaper and then betting on the horses. He is obsessed with winning at the track; all his thoughts and dreams involve winning easy money. Shorty, who observes Karty every day, accurately diagnoses the problem as "a disease."

Karty also has an excitable, unpredictable temperament, another characteristic he shares with Coblenz. Like Coblenz, he is first presented in a maniacal frenzy. Karty flies off the handle when Shorty turns off the lights in the cellar at Ann's. Shorty is merely following Spitzbergen's orders; he doesn't know that Karty is down there, but the gambler erupts with anger. He has been studying the horses, and doesn't want to be disturbed. Karty has rid himself of familial obligations but he is not free, for he has enslaved himself to the races. Shorty is right; his obsession is like a sickness.

Karty's underground identity, then, is that of the outcast. He does not consciously pursue any ethic of freedom in Dostoevsky's sense (or even in Coblenz's sense), but merely removes himself from the normal routines of daily life. The intensity with which Karty approaches his gambling makes him a grotesque, which distinguishes him from Coblenz. Coblenz loves to gamble and, like everyone else, likes to win, but it never seems to be a life-and-death matter to him. The one time he does win, he gives away the money, which Karty would never do. Karty, on the other hand, always seems on the verge of a nervous breakdown. Everything he does, he does with a frenzy that borders on violence. Eventually he is to be overwhelmed by violence and blood.

Moe Karty was not always addicted to the races. He used to be a family man with a respectable job as an accountant. The Depression, however, has soured him on the possibilities of earning an honest dollar in America. This is the essence of Karty's revolt against society. He has seen its corruption and been victimized by its precariousness and no longer wants to work within its framework. In this regard he is like Dostoevsky's Raskolnikov, who also rebels against a corrupt society. Raskolnikov manifests his revolt by killing the pawnbroker, who represents to him the heart of this corrupt society; Spitzbergen represents essentially the same thing to Karty. Specifically, however, he represents the economic imbalance in America, the gap that exists between the "haves" and the "have-nots." Perhaps that is why Karty is always plaguing him and hanging around his store. Karty will eventually kill Spitzbergen, though his reasons and motives will differ from Raskolnikov's.

The similarity to Raskolnikov ends there, however. Raskolnikov is an intellectual with a Napoleonic complex (he dreams of a superior Raskolnikov who will be born when he outwits society); his ethic and life's plan are the result of much thought. He has reasoned out the notion of freedom and has decided to act it out and clinically observe the consequences. But Karty is no intellectual. He has no great objections to the money ethic of his society, if only he can have a lot of money; he merely does not want to acquire it in the normal way. Those who have money are the objects of Karty's spite. If he can get some, perhaps he will calm down. And he is determined to get money the easy way. He has worked out a formula for beating the odds which he is sure will net him a profit, but he needs a stake. During the course of the novel he spends a great deal of time trying to convince Spitzbergen, Shubunka, and Lurie that his plan is foolproof, hoping that they will give him the necessary funds. In one scene he desperately tries to convince Lurie that his plan will work. He calls it his "syndicate idea":

Play it my system and it's as good as an investment in the bank. Interest: that's what it is. . . . Five hundred from you, five from Shubunka and Spitz, I put in five and I play the horses on a progressive system with the two thousand. We can't lose. We'll make a fortune. (pp. 38–39)

No one, of course, is willing to give him the money, and Karty spends his time cursing fate, life, and his fellow man, and trying to avoid his wife. In between he bets with the little money he has, usually losing, because he can't help taking chances on the long shots. What he does win amounts to very little.

Karty is also in deep trouble with his wife's brothers. One morning Harry, one of the brothers, from whom Karty has embezzled $1,300, surprises Karty on the street and begins to beat him unmercifully, "with the satisfied, preoccupied expression of a man who is doing his job" (pp. 95–96). Harry works on Karty like one of the hired thugs of the earlier novels. The resemblance is significant for it fully exposes the callousness of man in the modern wasteland, where family means nothing, love is dead, money rules, and it is either pay up, kill, or be killed.

Fortunately Karty's wife intrudes and stops her brother. Mrs. Karty is the only really decent person in the novel. She is a minor character who doesn't figure significantly in the action of the book, but because of her goodness she makes her presence felt. Despite her husband's life-style, she never really abandons him, but is always worrying about him and urging him to take care of himself. Above all she is compassionate and forgiving, characteristics which Fuchs feels are sadly lacking in the modern age and which only Mrs. Karty seems to possess.

The fight attracts a crowd, and in a scene similar to one in *Summer in Williamsburg* (the fight between Mrs. Linck and Marge), people gather around the fighters to enjoy the action. No one attempts to stop the fight, for no one wants to ruin a good time. This crowd again reflects the plight of the masses (the lost tribe from Winesburg) in the modern world. Bored and dissatisfied, they will seize upon any form

of excitement (preferably violence) to break up the monotony of the
day. Finally an old man, watching the fight from his apartment
window, calls for the police, but it does no good. Disgusted and
outraged, the old man gives voice to the despair of the author,
lamenting the disease that has blighted Neptune Beach. The poor
man is only jeered at for his pains:

He took advantage of the occasion to deliver a lecture, impassionate and
burning, on the decencies of human life. Everyone quite forgot the fight to
hoot and yell up at the intellectual. (p. 97)

The old man's threat to throw down a pot of water disperses the
crowd, and Harry drags Karty into Ann's. Spitzbergen is outraged,
and his reaction is typical: "Is this a place for talking? It ain't my
business here for people to come in for talking. I don't pay rent for it."
Ignoring him, Harry slaps his brother-in-law around some more,
infuriating Mrs. Karty, who fights back, yelling, "You want to kill him
altogether for a couple of lousy dollars?" Her remark once again
underlines one of the novel's basic themes, the dehumanizing
influence that money has on people's lives.

Karty reacts to all of this with spite, one of his special characteristics
and one which he shares with the Underground Man and Coblenz:
"Go to hell, you bastard. Don't think I'm going to forget this in a
hurry. You'll get yours for this" (p. 100). His threats, of course, are
meaningless, for, like the Underground Man, he is too weak to carry
out any of the threats he makes against his enemies. Karty's spite is
even directed against his wife who has saved him and again tries to
help him, urging him to return the money. Karty's response is
typical: "Go away. Go to hell. Leave me alone."

Karty, left alone, ponders his own private trap, "Where could he
go, how could he escape? It was a miserable world." As time moves
inexorably against him, he will discover that there is indeed no
escape, as he is pushed further and further into the corner.

IV *Shubunka*

The creation of Shubunka was considered, by those critics who
reviewed the novel, to be Fuchs's finest achievement in the book. In
1937 the *New York Times* said, "Fuchs' finest characterization is
lavished on a huge and hideous hulk of a man named Shubunka."[13]

Howard Moss, reviewing the first three novels when they were reissued in 1961, said of *Low Company* that "Shubunka is the real invention here,"[14] and Alfred Kazin labeled him "Mr. Fuchs' prize creation."[15]

Shubunka is indeed a "prize creation." Although he is one of many such creations in the novel, he is the one that is felt most deeply. His plight is more moving and his cries more touching than those of people like Moe Karty.

Shubunka, too, is a grotesque, as is manifested most obviously in his extreme ugliness:

His was a huge face, his jaws like slabs of meat, black with his beard no matter how often he shaved. His thick black hair, combed straight to the side, was heavily greased with Polymol . . . his big face, lumpy nose and gross lips, the black line running unbroken across his eyes rendered him completely ugly, his face on his short thick neck then looking unnatural, like nothing human. (p. 55)

His physical appearance separates him from others, who find him repulsive and somewhat frightening. Shubunka is aware of this and it hurts him. He has a certain sensitivity and displays at times a genuine affection for people (he is the only major character who seems capable of a generous gesture), but he is usually rebuffed. Deep down he is a lonely man who yearns for companionship. His ugliness, his fat shape, and his "waddling" gait make him awkward, and his attempts at communication generally fail. People do not respond to his overtures.

When first presented, he is mingling with the people at Ann's. When Herbert Lurie tells him that he is engaged to Dorothy, the cashier at Ann's, Shubunka is touched. He likes Dorothy and wants to give her some money as a wedding gift. Dorothy, however, both afraid and repelled by Shubunka, refuses the gift. Shubunka is hurt, but in the hurt there is a touch of self-pity, a feeling that Shubunka indulges often. This characteristic, and the almost narcissistic obsession with his own ugliness which prompts him in this moment of rejection to seek out a mirror "to catch a glimpse of his face when it showed sorrow," relieve the pathos of his situation and check the sympathy that the portrayal of his unhappiness often creates.

Shubunka, despite his appearance, is tolerated at Ann's because of his money, as he is aware.

He knew that every time he walked into Ann's they all looked away from him, they wouldn't come near him because he was funny looking, and they hated him, because they saw his clothes and the money he had. . . . . But in spite of them he had built up an organization that made money for him almost automatically. Let them all rot in hell. He had the money and they would come to him whether they wanted to or not. (p. 63)

This economic reality Shubunka learned at an early age. Like Karty he knows that in America fortunes are not made by working with one's hands, but by selling something to people, "something they really wanted, something they would be willing to pay for well" (pp. 56–57). What he sells them is a good time; he is a small-time operator of houses of prostitution. Like the movie people in *The Day of the Locust*, Shubunka is a purveyor of dreams. He gives the people what they want, what Claude Estee, a character in West's novel, aptly calls "amour and glamor." This is precisely the dream of many of the people whose lives are so dull that they come to Neptune Beach seeking excitement.

Shubunka, while succeeding in alleviating the loneliness of others, is unable to help himself. The emptiness of his life becomes greater when an unknown mob invades Neptune Beach, eliminating all the small-time whore-house operators. Shubunka is told to give up his business and leave town. He is also threatened through Spitzbergen, who is told to stop dealing with him. All of his employees and contacts are also threatened, and Shubunka, who once felt secure in his business, finds himself ignored by all of his former associates. He is a marked man, and people are afraid to be seen with him. While the people around him take this new organization seriously, Shubunka, at first, dismisses it as the work of "a couple of cheap bums" (pp. 87–88). Their methods, however, give him pause, and he is soon to suffer the consequences of resistance. Later, when a policeman whom he regularly bribes refuses his money, he realizes how alone he is. The ways of *his* world become very clear to him:

It was bitter and low, humans were always miserable in their relations with one another, but it was an old tale, he knew it and could not be shocked. Now he was stripped of all vanity, all affectation, only a simple man left to his grief. (p. 92)

Shubunka's remorse is not really sincere, however, and this apparent self-realization is not to be trusted. He enjoys feeling sorry for himself, and these moments of self-laceration comfort him and make him feel superior to others (particularly those at Ann's) who he feels are not as sensitive as he is. Fuchs emphasizes this characteristic later in the novel, when, again alone and feeling down, Shubunka seemingly repents, but Fuchs undercuts his seeming sincerity:

Shubunka smoked his cigarette lying on the bed, solaced by his reflections, for they contained the right elements to draw pity and understanding from his imaginary audience and he knew it. . . . The image of himself in his mind's eye soothed him. (p. 254)

Shubunka is really a fake. In following the forms of repentance, he never really recognizes the value of goodness, nor does he ever indicate that he will change. He regrets his evil ways because his life has finally boomeranged on him and he is being punished. Even the punishment (at least up to this point) is not enough to make him change his ways, because after each of these private confessionals, he picks himself up and continues his old way of life.

Now, alone, and threatened by the organization, he becomes afraid. He visits Herbert Lurie and invites him to lunch. Walking along the beach, he opens his heart to Lurie in a painful, muffled cry for help. The talk is interrupted by the appearance of two thugs who want Shubunka. He is told to get out of town, "or it will be the last mistake you ever make in your life." Shubunka begs them to be considerate, telling them that he is a simple man and doesn't want to bother the syndicate. One of the thugs, repelled by the sight of Shubunka, is aching to punch him and finally does:

The thug was in a fury and slapped the fat man heavily on the cheeks. . . . The prize-fighter kept on cracking Shubunka with his palm and finally shoved him backward. He fell to the sand, jarring his head as he hit the ground. He lay still, his eyes opened in fear, rigid. The hat fell off his painstakingly combed hair, which now grew disheveled. (p. 149)

The description is similar to that of the violent scene between Karty and his brother-in-law. In *Low Company* the violence which has been in the background of all of Fuchs's novels is unleashed with full force.

Shubunka becomes wild with grief. He gets hysterical and begins crying to the thugs:

What am I? A dog? You have no right to do this! It is not the way for one human being to treat another! . . . We must not be like animals to each other! We are human beings all together in this world. Please! I beg you." (p. 151)

His pleading for human treatment is touching even as it is ironic. It is Fuchs's ultimate comment that this plea for human decency should come from a man who is trying to defend small-time prostitution against organized crime. Later, alone in his room, Shubunka learns the meaning of silence and of real, total loneliness as he waits, desperately wanting to see or hear from someone, anyone: "He grew filled with foreboding that no one was calling him now. It was as though he were dead" (p. 187). It is a moving scene—the marked man isolated, hoping to hear from someone, turning on the radio to keep out the silence. It is a vivid portrait of a caged man. Finally, in desperation, he calls someone, only to be hung up on.

Now he feels bad that he didn't lend money to Moe Karty and decides to give him some: "It was the least one human could do for another." This insight and seeming desire to change direction is again only temporary. His thoughts carry him back to his days of poverty, "of his work in the wicker business, of the counting of pennies and nickels when he had his candystand. . . ." He recalls how he built up his present business and relishes his position of wealth. He decides to fight, not to give up what it has taken him so long to build: "I won't go. Let them kill me. Let them shoot me. I won't give up." Old values die hard. Shubunka can't abandon them.

V *Tiresias*

Herbert Lurie, the dress-shop proprietor, while not a really prominent character, assumes a certain importance as Fuch's conscience and mouthpiece in the novel. An intelligent man, he is well fitted to comment upon the events and the characters, and he functions both as an observer and as a participant in the action. Like Tod Hackett in *The Day of the Locust*, Lurie touches the lives of all the major characters in the novel. He is a daily visitor to Ann's and knows Spitzbergen very well. Karty is familiar enough to ask him for a loan, and he knows Shorty well enough to see through his poses. Shubunka also attaches himself to Lurie and opens up to him. When Shubunka is beaten up on the beach, it is Lurie who witnesses the action. What he sees makes him feel "deathly sick."

He is intelligent enough to understand Neptune Beach, and, speaking to Shubunka, he voices Fuchs's sentiments when he says:

The boys at Ann's. Yes, I know what you mean. No feeling. No heart. They live their own selfish way and they have no room in their heart for another, for his hopes and desires, for his disappointment and tragedy. They are hard as stones, their hearts. (p. 145)

As an observer, an intelligent seer, Lurie functions as a kind of Tiresias figure in the novel. His remark about the hardened hearts of Neptune Beach links him to the Tiresiases both of *Oedipus Rex* and *The Waste Land*. In Sophocles's play it is Tiresias who recognizes that the curse which has come upon the Theban land is the result of the sinful relationship of Oedipus and Jocasta. Oedipus's sin, however, was committed in ignorance, while the sins witnessed by the Tiresias figure in Eliot's poem and by Lurie in *Low Company* are not committed in ignorance, nor, as Shubunka's thoughts reveal, are they regarded as sins at all. Lurie walks through a land of beasts.

VI *You Can't Beat the Races*

As in the earlier novels, Fuchs at last ties the lives of his protagonists together, here uniting them in a common bond of destruction. In the final section of the novel all rush headlong to their dooms, as their lives of abomination boomerang on them.

Shorty's fate is the mildest by comparison, but still it is unsettling when he is fully exposed for what he really is. The exchange of letters with Madame Pavlovna has finally produced a date, and Shorty is determined to make it a night to remember. After a dinner at "the Chinks," some talk, and a frustrating time at the movies, where the corsetière rebuffs his attempts to caress her, Shorty finally gets Madame Pavlovna up to her apartment. Here things go from bad to worse. He persuades her to get into "something more comfortable," while he prepares the living room for romance. He turns down the lights and looks for some music, finally having to settle for "On the Volga," a solo by Richard Tauber.

When the Madame appears, she makes a movie-star entrance, attired in "a black chiffon negligee tied at the side with a green sash" (pp. 245–46). Shorty is wild with desire. They sit on the couch and Shorty makes his move. The scene, however, is more reminiscent of a wrestling match than love-making. It is akin to the earlier scenes of violence; Fuchs describes the action with violent words and images. In the world of Neptune Beach there is little difference between gang-beatings and love-making. Here even love is violent and evil.

When Madame Pavlovna finally tells him that she does not want to be treated like this, that she had a platonic affair in mind, Shorty,

angered, attacks her again. In a rather Kafkaesque scene the corsetière turns into a masculine, looming giant and physically throws
Shorty out of the apartment:

She raised herself from the sofa with extraordinary strength, exploding into a
burst of cries and curses. As she rose, she lifted Shorty outspread in the air.
. . . Beside his short form she seemed a giantess. Shorty couldn't catch his
breath. She had him fixed fast with the fingers of his hair in one hand while
she slapped his face wtih strength, each blow stinging until the tears came to
his eyes. She went on whacking him, tripping and falling over him, dragging
him to the door as she belabored him. Here she almost picked him up bodily
and threw him into the narrow hall. . . .
    The corsetière towered over him, her chest heaving. She drew her
negligee carefully over her and looked down at him with enormous con-
tempt.
    "Cockroach," she said, and slammed the door. (p. 251)

Disgusted and humiliated, Shorty returns to Ann's, vowing he will
be a nice guy no longer. He decides that he will have a woman that
night no matter what and talks Lillian, the cashier, into going down to
the basement with him. He attacks her, animallike in his furious
embraces. Lillian screams and tries to resist, and finally, disgusted
with it all, Shorty lets her go, defeated again.

As the night draws to a close, Shorty is alone with no place to go. He
begins to envy the "relief man," the man who replaces him when he is
off. Throughout the book the "relief man" (another nameless soul) is
described as someone at peace with himself. He never gets involved
in anything, never really participates in life, and as a result never gets
excited or hurt. Shorty decides that this philosophy of withdrawal is
the one that any sensible man should adopt:

That was the best way of doing things, three-quarters dead, because then you
had no inclinations and you were never disappointed, never got kicked in the
teeth. (p. 294)

Shorty walks off into the night a defeated, bald, and repulsive man.
He is really nothing more than a "cockroach."

Karty is up to his head in trouble, in desperate need of that $1,300.
He persuades Arthur to steal some money from Spitzbergen's cash
register during a busy time in the store. In return he promises to take
Arthur with him to the race track. Arthur is excited about the

prospect of going to the track, but he is somewhat nervous about taking the money, and even more so about leaving his quiet life at Ann's. Despite his nervousness, and intimidated by Karty, Arthur steals the money. Karty, however, forces him to take twenty dollars instead of the planned ten. The difference is crucial to Arthur because he cannot replace the twenty with his weekly paycheck—it is more than he makes. In taking this money, Arthur pierces the "darkness." No longer viewing Ann's as a secure place, but as a "jail," he rushes out, after the theft, into the realm of experience.

Arthur's education widens once he reaches the race track. At first things go well: the world is new and Arthur is caught up in the excitement. Karty's first bet comes in, and they both feel that luck is with them. Fuchs undercuts the excitement, however, with Arthur's first view of the crowd. Once again Fuchs anticipates West in his understanding of the working of the masses:

To Arthur, sitting high in the stands, the crowd seemed to become a single unit, in constant motion but according to a definite pattern and design, like the ocean swell and fall, and this was so because the people streamed to their destinations in the same channels: rushing to the gambling ring and rushing away from it. . . . Everyone smoked cigars and everyone spat. . . . (pp. 164–65)

Arthur, whose empty life is representative of the lives of the people in Fuchs's crowd, is curious. He leaves his seat in the grandstand and goes down below to see the people and catch some of the excitement firsthand. Like Tod Hackett and Homer Simpson (and Max Balkan) he gets caught up in the crowd. Arthur gets to see the faces of these people: they have the stare of the cheated and betrayed—their eyes gleam with hatred; their faces are "grim and vicious" (p. 175).

This experience disturbs Arthur, and he tells Karty that he wants to go home. But Karty won't leave, for he is on a lucky streak, winning, and he can't stop now. He has a hunch and bets everything on a long-shot horse named Gillie. Gillie is Karty's "Latabelle," but unlike Coblenz's, Karty's long shot fails to come in. All is lost. Ruined and on the verge of tears, Karty is afraid to go home. To make matters worse, Arthur is upset about the money, sure that Spitzbergen has by now discovered the theft and that he will be caught. Karty calms him down by telling him that he will get the money from a friend.

Spitzbergen has indeed discovered the theft and is on the verge of a breakdown. He immediately blames the new cashier, who breaks

into tears while proclaiming her innocence. Spitzbergen is at his wits'
end; first his ice-cream machine is smashed, Shubunka hasn't paid
him two-weeks' rent money, and now twenty dollars is missing from
the cash register.

Meanwhile Karty's brothers-in-law are tracking him down. They
find him and take him and Arthur to the garage, where the brothers
beat up Karty again. The day is becoming a nightmare for Arthur.
After witnessing the beating he cries, "I'm going to vomit. I can't help
it. I'm sorry. I'm going to vomit." Karty is finally released after he
convinces his brothers-in-law that he will get the money that night.

Shubunka, too, is being hunted. Contrary to the orders of the
organization, he has not left town, because "without the prestige of
his money, he had nothing and might as well be dead" (p. 254). Now
some hired thugs are out to get him. That evening he gets a call from
someone in the organization offering him a job, and they make an
appointment to meet that night. It is a set-up; when Shubunka leaves
his apartment and steps outside, he narrowly escapes the bullets of
the mob's gunmen. He is spared, saved, condemned to go on. Alone,
and being tracked down like a hunted animal, he runs, finally arriving
at the boardwalk, where he hopes to lose himself among the people.
Like Poe's "Man of the Crowd" he begins to move with the masses,
but eventually the people disperse and Shubunka is once again alone.
He is panic-stricken. Where can he go? To whom can he turn?

Time passes and Karty and Arthur make their way back to Ann's.
For Arthur, Ann's has changed:

. . . the scene, glaringly brilliant amid the darkness of the other stores on the
avenue, became strangely unfamiliar, far away and unreal, as though he were
seeing it in a dream. (p. 259)

It is past midnight when Spitzbergen leaves Ann's for home. Karty,
with Arthur close behind, follows him. They take the same train and
get off at Spitzbergen's stop. Karty then follows Spitzbergen into the
bathroom and asks him for money. When Spitzbergen refuses, Karty
attacks him. Another fight begins; but this time Karty has the
advantage. He now uses on Spitzbergen the wrench that his
brothers-in-law used on him earlier:

. . . Spitzbergen squirmed and made retching noises. His hands were feebly
scratching at Karty's face, and soon they fell to his shoulders which he began
patting slowly and listlessly as a man would in talking to an old friend. Then

the squrming stopped, the choking noises stopped and the hands fell down to his sides, softly slapping the wall with the swing. (p. 289)

Spitzbergen, who has lived his whole life for money, is beaten to death for it. Dead in a subway station toilet, Spitzbergen the capitalist "forgot the cry of gulls, and the deep sea swell, and the profit and loss."

Arthur is outside while all this is happening. He has, however, learned something from his day's experiences:

What a sap he had been, feeling jealous of Karty and Shorty and Shubunka. They could have all the tough talk and ways. Arthur didn't want them. So he was a kid, so he didn't know nothing, so it was better. You had nothing on your mind and that was something money couldn't buy. (p. 283)

Unfortunately, however, Arthur now has learned too much, and lost the innocence that once protected him from a brutal world. When he discovers the murder he goes wild with fear and screams at Karty. The day has come to a violent end.

The emotional tension of the day's events have by now drained the reader as well as the characters. The death of Spitzbergen comes almost as a relief, functioning as a kind of release. But there is more. Shubunka has found his way to Lurie's new apartment, where he begs for shelter and protection. Lurie is touched by the man's pleas, but Dorothy, his fiancée, has unfortunately returned, and at the sight of Shubunka she is both repelled and angry. She insists that Lurie throw Shubunka out, but he refuses. He knows Shubunka is in trouble and tries to reason with Dorothy, "I can't tell him to go. . . . Those gangsters would kill him if they saw him." She won't listen and storms out of the house. Shubunka is upset that he has caused a quarrel and offers to leave, but Lurie insists that he stay. Suddenly Shubunka sees a large car pull up across the street, and he thinks that his time has come. Tired of running, he decides to die. He goes downstairs screaming: "Kill me. . . . It's a favor. I want it. What are you waiting for? Shoot already and make a finish of it." (p. 309)

It is a false alarm. The car is not occupied by assassins, but by two teenagers making love. But Shubunka now recognizes his defeat; he has lost all hope. He leaves Lurie and walks off into the night. This, Shubunka's exit from the novel, is touching. He is not a majestic figure, but a waddling, ugly, lonely man who has lost. In defeat he has gained some stature, for he has at least lost his self-pity, but it is not suggested that he has gained any self-knowledge, and nothing has been affirmed by his defeat. His "empire" of prostitution remains, though it is now run by organized crime. Neptune Beach is still a diseased land.

Shubunka's story has, however, touched the life of Herbert Lurie. This night especially has taught him a great deal. Watching Shubunka walk away, he experiences a moment of revelation:

> Witnessing the resignation of Shubunka as the man walked to the subway, realizing that he, too, had a conscience and recognized in his own peculiar way the justice of his fate, above all, feeling with pity his complete wretchedness, Lurie knew now that it had been insensible and inhuman for him, too, simply to hate Neptune and seek escape from it. This also was hard and ignorant, lacking human compassion. He had known the people at Ann's in their lowness and had been repelled by them, but now it seemed to him that he understood how their evil appeared in their impoverished lives and, further, how miserable their own evil rendered them. It was not enough to call them low and pass on. (p. 311)

Fuchs's compassion is here revealed in its full force through Lurie. Despite their lowness, he, too, refuses to abandon these people. He loves them and hopes to comfort them. For Daniel Fuchs this world is all and one must live in it and accept it. He offers no hopes for the future, no alternative plans of action. His concern is for the present, for that is all each man has.

The next day the sun comes out. It is hot and the people flock to the beaches. The papers carry the story of Spitzbergen's murder and the arrest of Karty and Arthur. The people are interested and amused by the story because it all happened so close to home. But it is a new day. To the proprietors it is a good day for business: there are lots of people to serve and plenty of money to be made.

The death of Spitzbergen and the destruction of the crowd at Ann's seem to have brought about the good weather. The debased god has been killed and life is temporarily back to normal at Neptune Beach. The final scene, however, merely emphasizes Fuchs's own theory that "people . . . lived in a circle without significance, one day the duplicate of the next until the end." Lurie will return to a Neptune Beach that is essentially the same; Spitzbergen, Karty, Arthur, and Shubunka may not be there, but others will replace them with similar aims and obsessions. Shubunka has already been re-placed; his departure does not mean the end of his business or of his way of life.

Richard H. Pells, writing about some of the "conservative" writers of the 1930s, says of Fuchs:

. . . One could find in the efforts of writers as different as Daniel Fuchs and William Faulkner a common emphasis on acceptance rather than action, tolerance rather than anger. . . .[16]

This novel is, indeed, "tolerant." Fuchs is not so much outraged at the distressing conditions of life as resigned to their eternal truth. Nevertheless, his novels are full of the humor, poignancy, and even occasionally the beauty that is present in the lives of ordinary men.

Implicit in *Low Company* and in the other two novels is a hope and a prayer. By exposing the sins of man, Fuchs hopes to make us aware. The picture is ugly, but there are still figures in it like Herbert Lurie, Mr. Hayman, and Max Balkan. The ultimate message of this last novel lies in the prayer that concludes Eliot's *Waste Land:* "Give, Sympathize, Control." Such actions are not often seen at Neptune Beach, but they are, nonetheless, man's birthright. It is the author's prayer that we embrace them, for without them mankind will always remain "low company."

CHAPTER 5

"Williamsburg in Technicolor"

Hollywood. . . .

When Fuchs arrived in Southern California in 1937, he found what appeared to be a dreamland:

> . . . the area is still undeveloped, so I am granted the boon of being in a new place, fresh and brimming and unawakened, at the beginning. There are masses of bougainvillea, Joshua trees and yucca on the hills, a light shining at the door, the scent of orange blossoms in the evening air, honeysuckle and jasmine. . . . I drive on my free days, through the Santa Susana Pass into the Simi Valley, or to the ranges of the San Gabriels and the deserts beyond them, or over great open spaces to the harbors of Wilmington and San Pedro—everything in this new land wonderfully solitary, burning and kind.[1]

It was as if the dream of America had been renewed, and once again one confronted the freshness and vitality of the frontier.

Dominating the lives of the people, their psyches, their visions, even to some extent the land itself, were the film studios: "The studios exude an excitement, a sense of life, a reach and hope, to an extent hard to describe."[2] It was for one of these studios that Daniel Fuchs came to work as a screenwriter in 1938.

Fuchs's attitudes toward Hollywood are complex and varied. Like other writers who have written of Hollywood, he exposes the emptiness and the waste that lie beneath the beauty, the sunshine, and the glamor, and yet he is not angry, bitter, or resentful, as many of the others have been. Fuchs, unlike any other distinguished novelist who worked in Hollywood, expresses a certain amount of respect for the movies, never writing of them as a debased medium or referring to himself as "a whore working in a brothel." In an essay written in 1961, Fuchs praises the artists who shaped the film industry:

116

They were a gaudy company, rambunctious and engrossed. What they produced, roistering along in those sun-filled, sparkling days was a phenomenon, teeming with vitality and ardor, as indigenous as our cars or skyscrapers or highways, and as irrefutable. Generations to come, looking back over the years, are bound to find that the best, most solid creative effort of our decades was spent in the movies, and it's time someone came clean and said so.[3]

Fuchs's essays about his experiences in Hollywood are stylistically unlike anything he had written before. They employ a stream of consciousness technique, and at times have an almost incoherent quality. Basically a series of impressions, anecdotes, and opinions, in the end the essays somehow fit together and achieve a kind of design. They are among his most beautifully written pieces and tell a great deal about Fuchs's attitudes toward the film industry.

The movies represent only part of the picture, however. There is that greater entity known as Hollywood, a place that encompasses the film industry but goes beyond it. It is a place with a personality of its own—like Williamsburg, it has its own topography, sounds, movements, and landscape. This larger phenomenon is what Fuchs explores in his Hollywood fiction, and it is here that Fuchs's darker vision is reborn. Williamsburg has now become a glittering city, bathed in a brilliantly clean sunshine; but beyond the attractive exterior, little has changed.

Much has been written recently about Hollywood fiction. Those critics who have attempted to define it as a genre have ascribed to it a set of characteristic themes (to be dealt with in detail later) which may pertain to it but do not necessarily distinguish the Hollywood novel from the novels of other American loci. Though they can certainly be found in many Hollywood novels, these same themes were explored by Fuchs earlier in the Williamsburg novels. Carolyn See has written that "the Hollywood novel . . . takes the whole of American history and the American dream as its province."[4] This is true, but for Fuchs's Jewish immigrants Williamsburg represented the American dream, and the lie behind that dream could be fully explored in the Williamsburg novels. Something more than the "American dream" must be at work in Fuchs's Hollywood fiction. The phrase perhaps is still applicable, but now it is a dream renewed, for California seems to make promises that were never offered in the East. The dream is somehow different now. Edmund Wilson wrote, "Everything that is wrong with the United States is to be found there in rare purity."[5]

Indeed everything about this place is pure and undiluted, as is exemplified and highlighted by its landscape, which makes Southern California somewhat different from other sections of the country, even as it accentuates its failure as a Utopia.

Southern California with its rolling hills, bright sunshine, and citrus groves, became in the aftermath of industrialism the ideal embodiment of Turner's words about America: ". . . the land of European dreams . . . where peace and happiness, as well as riches and eternal youth were to be found."[6] In Steinbeck's *The Grapes of Wrath*, when the Joads, like Moses, stand upon a mountain and view California for the first time, their vision is of a promised land. The scene is almost religious, reminiscent of the long-suffering pilgrims' first sight of the new Jerusalem:

"Jesus Christ! Look!" he said. The vineyards, the great flat valley, green and beautiful, the trees set in rows, and the farm houses.
And Pa said, "God Almighty!" The distant cities, the little towns in the orchard land, and the morning sun, golden on the valley. . . .[7]

Hopes and dreams like this made California "a permanent symbol of opportunity and freedom."[8]

Southern California has come to stand for many things, and the very name of the place arouses varied images in the mind. It may suggest a place where fortunes are made quickly and easily, or it may be seen as the ultimate expression of luxury and romance—a Jay Gatsby party magnified 100 times.

Hollywood is also Marilyn Monroe—a place that reeks with sexiness. This appeal is complex, for the Hollywood sex symbol, as Jonas Spatz points out, "was desirable not only because of her physical attributes but also because she appeared inseparable from the atmosphere of wealth and power that would necessarily accompany those who would claim her favor."[9]

All of these qualities are of course exaggerated and perpetuated by Hollywood's chief product, the movies. Thus reflected and magnified in its own image machine, Southern California seems a world apart, part of America yet different and divided from it. An atmosphere of unreality hangs about it, making a nowhere world that is somehow outside the normal flux of events. Edmund Wilson explains that this atmosphere of unreality stems partly from the climate:

. . . the empty sun and the incessant rains; and of landscape: the dry mountains and the void of the vast pacific; of the hypnotic rhythms of day and night that revolve with unblurred uniformity, and of the surf that rolls up the beach with a beat that seems expressionless and purposeless after the moody assaults of the Atlantic.[10]

This effect can be powerful, and Hollywood writers often emphasize the weather and physical surroundings to heighten their themes of artificiality and decay.

The weather, the physical environment, the movies, the life-style, the newness—all made California different, special. It represented a new world when there seemed to be no space left in the "new world." It is to this place that Fuchs's characters have come. In Williamsburg life was too full of the real, the commonplace; the ideal was only to be dreamed about or imagined, certainly not experienced. Hollywood, or Southern California, with its magic, its special differences, seems to promise to change that, to bridge the gap between reality and those ideals that had proved so unreachable elsewhere. As Carolyn See writes, "Hollywood is a place where people have a chance to be—somehow—their ideal selves."[11]

Perhaps the ideal can be experienced. It is a staggering promise, and one to be clutched at all the more desperately after the failure that Williamsburg represented. But California, too, proves a failure, and Hollywood fiction is an exposé, a record and a reaction to that failure. For Fuchs Hollywood is nothing more than "Williamsburg in Technicolor." The journey from coast to coast has been completed; there is "nothing new under the sun."

In addition to the essays (views from which will be incorporated into the discussion of the fiction), Fuchs wrote a novel and a number of short stories that treat of Hollywood. The stories can be divided into two groups: those that deal directly with the film industry, and those that deal with "landscape"—the life-style, climate, and people of Southern California. Certainly the shadow of the movies hovers over these lives, too, but in this second group Fuchs, as in the earlier novels, acts as an observer of everyday human behavior, commenting on an entire social milieu, rather than on the hectic, absurd, and frenzied activity of life in the movie studios.

The best of the stories dealing with the film industry was written early in Fuchs's Hollywood years. "A Hollywood Diary" (1938)[12] is a kind of Kafkaesque tale, rich in absurdist humor. Derived from a real diary which Fuchs kept when he first arrived in Hollywood, the story recounts in the first person the experiences of a young writer from the East who comes to California on contract to a film studio, and goes to start his first job. He arrives at his office "promptly at nine" and is eager to start work, which makes him suspect in the eyes of his less ambitious colleagues. This desire for work, however, is all the writer has, for despite the fact that he has been hired and is being paid, he is given no work, and "Himmer, my agent, tells me I'm getting 'beans' and have no reason to think of the waste of money." Although this kind of situation is certainly absurd, seasoned Hollywood veterans such as the agent Himmer find nothing unusual about it. Fuchs's young writer, however, has not yet been initiated, and he worries about not working. He wanders through the city:

In the evening I walk down Hollywood Boulevard with the other tourists, hoping for a glimpse of Carole Lombard and Adolphe Menjou. And after I get tired of walking I drop into a drugstore, where with the lonely ladies from Iowa, I secretly drink a thick strawberry soda.

Once again Fuchs anticipates West's descriptions of the bored and desperate people who come from the Midwest seeking excitement in California. His screenwriter, like West's crowd, finds no excitement.

Finally he gets an assignment to write a treatment of a story called "No Bread to Butter." The writer is delighted to be working, though it costs him status in the eyes of his colleagues. He writes the treatment quickly, and is told that working fast is bad policy. The script handed in, he waits weeks before the producer finally sees him, only to reject the script: "It's fine, it's subtle and serious. It's perfect—for Gary Cooper, not for my kind of talent." Quality counts for nothing, and the writer who is beginning to catch on, is not "especially depressed."

The absurd routine of studio life rolls on. He spends a lot of time now playing cards, taking long lunch breaks, and killing time. His final assignment is with a big producer named Kolb, who makes formula pictures and is very successful. The writer works on the script, hands it in, and again hears nothing. His attitude, however, has changed, for Hollywood no longer bothers him. He finally learns that Kolb has fired him because he is only a $200-a-week man and "Kolb figures he deserves the best writers on the lot." The cycle runs full circle when on July 15 he returns to his office to find his desk occupied by a new, anxious, and ambitious young writer. The narrator cleans up his desk and leaves.

This absurd tale of initiation into the crazy and bewildering studio world reflects Daniel Fuchs's first impressions of Hollywood. In

Hollywood everything was upside down—the abnormal became the norm. The most amazing thing to Fuchs, however, was not the craziness, but that despite the confusion, the movies managed to get made:

The wonder was the picture. It was whole now, sound—the myriad nervelines of continuity in working order, the conglomeration of effects artfully rejuggled, brisk and full of urgent meaning.[13]

This feeling of mystery, that order could be and was produced from chaos, underlies many of Fuchs's attitudes toward his Hollywood experience. He never really tries to analyze how Hollywood worked, but seems awestruck and helpless before it. Hollywood then was a combination of energies, or to use Dreiser's phrase, "chemisms," mysterious forces that worked wonders and finally achieved its ends.

"Ecossaise, Berceuse, Polonaise,"[14] the first of the "landscape stories," deals with the emptiness of the lives of the very rich. It is filled with local-color details that emphasize the languid artificiality of the world that the wealthy inhabit. Mr. Keef is planning to give a party. He is about to remarry and wants to impress his bride with his friends, and the friends with her.

Mr. Keef has been married four times, and his fiancée, Mrs. Restes, "had been married a few times too." A characteristic emphasis of Hollywood fiction is on the death of love and normal sexuality. Fuchs has noted this before, in Williamsburg, but his Hollywood stories stress even more strongly the devaluation of marriage itself and the decline of decent human relationships. Divorces abound in these stories, and there is not even one happy marriage in all of Fuchs's Hollywood fiction.

This loss of love is at the core of Hollywood's moral climate, though the blight is effectively hidden by the physical landscape. Fuchs's opening description reveals a wonderland bathed in beauty, an Edenic landscape, a place where time is suspended. Behind the glitter, however, is sterility and nothingness. If the movement from East to West has been to find a land of beauty, wealth, pleasure, and eternal youth, perhaps this "manifest destiny" has been achieved. But a price has been paid—man has again abandoned honor, character, and dignity, and he has remained "low."

Mr. Keef's whole life is bound up in the pursuit of pleasure, the ethic of Southern California. He has no real moral fiber and he lacks the ability to understand his world or his life. After four marriages he

still feels that he can capture "the ideal" in a human relationship. His
fiancée likes to take long walks (born of the need in Southern
California to exercise and stay eternally young and beautiful), and he
goes with her:

Mr. Keef gamely played along. He sincerely wanted to do his best to keep
their courtship on a youthful, idyllic plane, but he was roly-poly and bald and
no athlete, and the hikes exhausted him.

The reality of his body intrudes: his "thighs chafe" and he is getting
old. Even in California one cannot arrest the progress of time.

While Mr. Keef embodies Southern California society, his daughter Kittysue represents a reaction against it. During the course of the
story she is being pursued by Tom, a neighbor. She has little patience
with him, however, for he is too much like the others—a typical
Beverly Hills product. She is very young and her reactions to her
environment take the form of childish acts of rebellion. She draws a
balloon on the living-room ceiling and in it writes the word "phooey."
Later, during the party, Tom sees the word "Blah" scribbled across
the pages of an open book.

The party takes up most of the story's action, providing Fuchs an
opportunity to expose Southern California society in a very cinematic
sequence: he trains his camera-eye on one group of people for a brief
time and then quickly cuts to another group. Only brief glimpses of
these people are given, but their actions and their words reveal a
great deal about them. Providing quick impressions of various
figures, Fuchs builds a collage effect that analyzes as it depicts the
whole scene. Moving from Vera, who is always changing the color of
her hair, to Mrs. Brutershaw, who is "telling the group around her
about a certain Mrs. Rogers, her regular personal astrologer," the
camera then picks up Mr. Brutershaw, who addresses his hearer as
"cherie," and an instant later, in another part of the room, zeroes in
on the Fleckshorns, who are "still painfully trying to save their
marriage." The party scene presents an assemblage of Hollywood
grotesques. These people live only for pleasure, continually indulg-
ing in fads—they are selfish, morally bankrupt. It is a modern-day
Gomorrah flourishing on the West Coast.

Kittysue understands all of this. During the evening she complains
to Tom, ". . . They're so horrible. . . . I hate them! Phooey! . . .
Phooey on them all! I hate them, every single one." Kittysue's
pronouncements disturb Tom. He proceeds to get drunk, and then

sick, and finally passes out. When he wakes up the next morning he finds himself still in the Keef house, being watched over by Dietz, Kittysue's younger sister. Dietz is overweight and ungainly, but the sight of her moves Tom to compassion, his first moment of true feeling.

Here is how Fuchs concludes the story:

> The leaves fluttered in the breeze, and so the sunshine, coming through the leaves, played and flickered on the wall in gentle, silent patterns . . . and lying on the piano, like a bittersweet remembrance of a time that now seemed gone forever, were the classical music pieces, the études and sonatas, the preludes, the lullabies and dances.

The piano and the music, to which Fuchs draws attention a number of times during the story, are symbols of a lost past, a better time when human feelings could take beautiful form, an age not stale and flat like this one. A civilization that could produce classical pieces, études, and sonatas is juxtaposed to Hollywood, the modern culture, which deserves only Kittysue's comment—"Phooey."

"Twilight in Southern California,"[15] Fuchs's most widely anthologized story, though hardly his best, elaborates this theme of emptiness. Alexander Honti is an immigrant who came to California many years ago, building up a novelty business (a suitable caricature of the film industry) and making enough money to put on an impressive show. Like everyone else in Beverly Hills, he displays the possessions that signal success—the big house, the swimming pool, a neurotic dog. When the story opens Honti is down on his luck, for "the novelty business was shot to pieces." The loan company has already taken away his car, and his debts are growing.

The action is set at the Hontis' swimming pool: Honti has invited some friends over to talk and lounge around the pool. Two of the guests are Morley and Barbara Finch, a young couple who have recently moved to Los Angeles from New Hampshire. Morley is Honti's doctor, and has become friendly with him. Barbara dislikes the Hontis and their crowd and detests the weekly visits to their home, but she goes anyway because of her husband, who is interested in precisely those things about the Hontis which Barbara dislikes. Like Herbert Lurie of *Low Company*, Morley continually analyzes the people around him, but whereas Lurie was repelled by the "lowness" of the people of Neptune Beach, Morley finds that he likes the Los Angeles types with their "peculiar ways."

The other guest is a man named Oleam, who "was also in the novelty business, also in distressed financial circumstances, but in addition his wife had left him and he had a stiff neck." Once again a broken marriage signals a wider social decay; the other relationships in the story are not very good either: the Hontis don't get along very well and the Finches are having problems. Oleam is sick over his wife's desertion. He is still very much in love with her, and has always been extremely jealous. Mrs. Honti has little patience with Oleam's sniveling, and points out that his life with his wife was hell, and he should be glad to be rid of her.

This is the kind of talk that has been going on before the Finches arrive. When Mrs. Honti sees the Finches approaching, she cautions:

Be still. . . . Now behave yourself. Watch how you talk—you will frighten her. She is a child. She comes from New Hampshire.

The remark is significant, for it points up the difference between Barbara Finch and the rest of the people. Morals are different in Southern California; the traveler from a more traditional part of the country will feel uncomfortable and out of place here. Morley's desire to be part of the group and Barbara's hatred of it forms the conflict of values at the center of the story.

Alexander Honti is Fuchs's portrait of the grotesque Southern California *nouveau-riche.* He is modeled on Shubunka, and the two have very much in common. Both are fat and repulsive (Fuchs describes Honti as a "punchinello, a gargoyle"), and their physical appearance creates a communications barrier between them and other people. Honti is basically a good man, but his desire to please, the smile-and-handshake pose that he lives by, has warped his personality. His efforts at being gracious jar with his appearance, and Barbara can't stomach him.

When he arrives home for the party he is immediately taken by the sight of Barbara, but he knows that she doesn't like him, and this makes him uncomfortable. Later he approaches her anyway, and the scene resembles one between Shubunka and Dorothy in *Low Company:*

Honti had climbed out of the pool and was heading directly for Barbara. He grabbed at her hand. She wouldn't let him have it. She shrank back and fidgeted. She didn't know what he was after, and she was, poor thing, frightened by him as he swarmed all over her. He was so big and hairy, the water sluicing off him, and without his glasses he squinted horribly. . . . She gave a shriek and bolted.

Her husband is concerned and embarrassed. He goes to Barbara and tries to comfort her, but she can only say, "They're depraved! They're degenerate." It is her judgment of the whole Southern California culture and society. Morley is confused, and his thought process reveals the ambiguity that underlies the experience of many in Southern California:

In the stillness now, he felt lost and his heart ached—because his wife looked lovely, because it was true, after all, that Honti was ugly and repellent, and because the sunlight over everything was so clear and brilliant.

Everything appears so beautiful. One is attracted to the land, even to the artificial, beautiful lives of the people. But it is really a false paradise, an area surrounded by a Circe-like curse. The people are Honti-like, they have become swine. Beneath the "clear and brilliant sunshine," things are "ugly and repellent." Morley longs to embrace the beauty and ignore the reality of things.

This mood is temporarily shattered by a commotion in the house. Brewer, Honti's designer, who has been in the hospital with a stroke, has called to say that he will be able to work. Honti feels that fortune has once again come his way and his hopes soar. In his excitement ("some devil got hold of him"), he pinches Barbara, and she slaps him hard, "in one blow destroying three hundred and fifty dollars' worth of bridgework on his lower jaw." The smack brings him back down to earth, deflating the dream of grandeur.

The party breaks up. Morley and his wife, angry at each other, drive home. Honti, too, takes a drive, during which he thinks longingly of his youth, and like Shubunka, reflects on his sinful life. His lines echo *Low Company:*

"Forgive me!" Honti suddenly said, pleading quietly but with all his heart and soul . . . Yes it was his fault. He had trespassed, he had transgressed; he had committed abominations, stretched the truth and kited checks.

The story ends with another description of the awesome beauty of the land, a majesty which dwarfs man and emphasizes his insignificance. This land, the final frontier, offered so much hope and promise, but man could not take advantage of its bounty. Again he has transgres-

sed. Now he has destroyed the final hope and promise by his inability
to be anything more than human.

"The Golden West"[16] again deals with the Hollywood social scene,
but this time Fuchs concentrates on movie people at a time when the
studio system is crumbling. The landscape, yet oblivious to the
change, still suggests wonder, romance, Utopia:

The California sunshine continued to pour down. The streets, the stucco
mansions, the lawns and the shrubbery sparkled with light.

And the people, accustomed to the old days and perhaps softened by
the sun, refuse to acknowledge that the dream, the promise, has
collapsed and gone unfulfilled.

This story, like the others, takes place on a Beverly Hills estate
where a party is being given. The host is Charles Spogel, an
accountant who "was also in the movie business." His brother-in-law
is Julian Vencie, "a top producer in the industry," now no longer
attached to a studio and having difficulties. Unemployment is not his
only problem: he is having difficulties with his wife, a simpleminded
starlet type (later it is revealed that she is having an affair), and a deal
he made with a studio has fallen through. Vencie had formed a
partnership with Boris Kittershoy (who has invested all of his wife's
money) in an independent film project, "largely on assurances given
to them by an executive at a major studio," but Vencie was not
helping his company improve its prospects—he is irrational and
temperamental and doesn't get along with the money people. Boris
Kittershoy calls him "a mass of contradictions" and adds that "nobody
can get along with him." As a result their company is out $200,000
with "no place to go."

Vencie has his origins in Schulberg's Sammy Glick. His mother,
who lives with the Spogels (Mrs. Spogel is Vencie's sister), is very
proud of her son's success, and her memories of her Julie link him to
Glick:

When he was a boy . . . when we lived on the East Side, you know what he
did? He walked! He couldn't stand the tenements—the babies crying, the
dumbwaiters, the garbage. He would walk for miles and miles, making up
dreams in his head, having ambitions. He would go and find a dime and ride
on the Fifth Avenue bus—he couldn't live if he didn't look at the fancy stores,
at the rich people!"

Vencie did manage to achieve success, but now must watch it crumbling, unable to save himself or salvage those ambitions.

The story centers on the social turmoil of the party. The Spogels and the Kittershoys are anxious for Julie and his wife, Imogene, to reconcile, but their efforts blow up in their faces. Vencie has learned about his wife's infidelity and embarrasses her in public. The atmosphere of the party is hectic, as people constantly run from place to place worrying about one thing or another. Finally a calm descends; everything has turned out badly—Vencie is without wife or a job, Imogene Vencie is distraught, and the Kittershoys are broke.

Only old Mrs. Vencie seems unaffected by all the turmoil, the fights, and the trouble. She had a hard life in New York: her husband, a furrier, "had caught the furriers' lung disease and had been totally incapacitated." One of her children was killed when he fell off the roof of an apartment building.[17] Now in California, in her old age, she feels rejuvenated, overwhelmed, and excited by the whirl, the glitter, the constant actitivy. The story ends as she talks to David, the narrator, who is also a guest at the party. Excited as she looks out and sees all the lights, she reminisces about the past and her husband:

Poor Papa. . . . You should have seen him when he was alive, David. He was elegant. He had a Kaiser Wilhelm mustache, with the points—a prince! On Sunday morning, he bought the breakfast, and if you asked him what did the whitefish cost, the carp, he never knew. He was too aristocratic to ask the storekeeper the price—he just paid the whole bill.

This description echoes Philip Hayman's account of his father in *Summer in Williamsburg*. Again Fuchs refers to an elegance that once was, but has disappeared from this flat age. Mr. Vencie, like Mr. Hayman, was a man with values, a very elegant man indeed. His type is no more. His son, the successful Hollywood producer, with all his money, lacks this elegance, and the moral fiber that it represents for Mrs. Vencie. She is enough of a realist to know that "nothing was out of the ordinary, that hopes were betrayed, that you always started out with illusion," and yet Southern California still fills her with a sense of awe: " 'Isn't it gorgeous?' she said to me. 'It's like a fairy-land, David. It's like magic!' "

This is the magic, the lure of the place: it still offers so many possibilities, it is so full of wonder. Here even the aged and the disillusioned can dream anew; here the promise of America has been renewed. But the movie industry is collapsing, Julian Vencie is desperate, the Kittershoys have failed, and Fuchs's "Golden West" continues to hide the quiet desperation of its inhabitants beneath the brilliant sunshine.

I   A Dry Heave

West of the Rockies, Fuchs's Hollywood novel, appeared in 1971, thirty-four years after his last published novel, *Low Company.* Aside from his screen work and an occasional short story, the literary world heard little from him after he left New York for Hollywood in 1937. Certain ghosts had come out of the closet in 1961 when Basic Books republished the Williamsburg novels in a single volume. Once again they were well received, but the book came and went quietly. His considerable talent, though recognized by some, was still not given the attention it deserved.

The arrival of *West of the Rockies* was a welcome event to that "small group of admirers"[18] who have always appreciated the Williamsburg novels; the book jacket called the appearance of Fuchs's novel "a greatly welcome event in American letters." The critics, however, were less kind. The book, on the whole, was not well received, the only Fuchs novel to be given more poor or mixed reviews than favorable ones. Irving Howe, always an admirer, was the only critic to give the book a wholehearted endorsement: "Simply as a writer of narrative, he is more skillful than ever."[19] Richard Ellman, on the other hand, found *West of the Rockies* lifeless:

Fuchs warns his readers away from experience like a father telling his son not to hang around with fast girls. If he has ever lived, he's not telling anybody about that here.[20]

The book is neither as good as Mr. Howe would have it, nor as bad as Mr. Ellman tried to make it sound. It is, to be sure, a rather uneven book. There are, as Howe implies, moments of splendid poetic writing; the novel's concluding passage is a good example:

The reporters, the technicians surged about, all this in a time already gone by, the events recounted here having taken place some twelve years ago, when television was comparatively new and the big picture studios still throbbed, the collapse yet to come, the people enmeshed in their concerns, those pursuits, dreams, and diversions which occupy us so that we are each of us precious to ourselves and wouldn't exchange ourselves, the being in us, with any other, those wonderful moments which as they happen go by almost unnoticed but which return again and again in our thoughts to bemuse and warm us, the stir of smoking mountain panoramas, the ache of sweet summer days, of trees in leaf, or being in love, this prize, this treasure, this phantom life.[21]

As Stanley Kauffman points out, Fuchs has "the ability to put the ephemeral into phrases that, paradoxically, fix their emphemeralness."[22] Phrases like "the stir of smoking mountain panoramas" manage to summon up for the reader the sense of the ephemeralness of life, which is a major theme in Fuchs's writing. The writing is also, as Howe points out, "compact" and "nervously taut," suggesting the immediacy and the critical nature of the heroine's dilemma.

The characters, at least the two leading ones, unfortunately do not command very much interest. Adele Hogue, while she is believable, is too much the clichéd successful-actress-neurotic type to be really compelling as a character. We have seen or read about her type before, and Fuchs does not give the character any new twists or dimensions that would make her more than a stock figure. Burt Claris also is too flat a character. He has his roots in other Fuchs *luftmenchen*, but never achieves any real status on his own. It is this lack of any sustained power in the creation of the leading characters that ultimately robs the book of the force and power that it could have achieved with a more sharply defined and realized center.

The novel, however, does have many merits, and it would be facile to dismiss it. As a portrait of human dissolution and decay it is effective, and it deserves further attention as part of the subgenre that has come to be called "the Hollywood novel." Considered in this context, the book takes on certain dimensions that might otherwise be overlooked.

Walter Wells, in his regional study of Hollywood fiction of the 1930s, perceptively ascribes certain common characteristics and themes to a group of Hollywood novels written in the 1930s. Discerning a body of literature of certain aesthetic significance that has drawn its setting from Southern California during the 1930s, Wells claims that in this literature "there emerges a complex yet remarkably consistent pattern of effects . . . which in toto define the Hollywood Southland literary region."[23] The characteristic that primarily shapes this kind of fiction is the theme of dissolution, "a generalized breaking down of the old, the traditional, the real, and the substantive."[24]

This and other characteristics which Wells ascribes to Hollywood fiction are evident in Fuchs's novel. (Though Wells's study deals with 1930s fiction, the characteristics he emphasizes apply equally well to many later Hollywood novels.) Among these supportive motifs is a general breakdown in human relationships. Man has lost the capacity to communicate, and instead "fear, envy and distrust dominate."[25] Language itself has also broken down: ". . . its meanings are often broadened beyond recognition, diluted by cliche, reversed, or otherwise distorted or blurred."[26] Beyond this, the literature reveals a loss of love and normal sexuality. The narrative action is speeded up, and "two dimensionality afflicts not only things but people."[27] Plot structures tend to be cinematic, and the books invariably employ first-person narration. Because of these characteristics Wells maintains that the works "possess an essential aesthetic affinity for each other. And that affinity is, for the most part, regional."[28]

Wells's theory is useful in examining Hollywood fiction, for although his formulas occasionally tend to limit his critical evaluations, he has succeeded in isolating the basic characteristics of a regional phenomenon. West of the Rockies exhibits many of these characteristics, and so it will be examined as an example of the "Hollywood novel" as well as in relation to Fuchs's earlier work.

West of the Rockies takes place in and around a Palm Springs hotel owned by Fannie Case. The place is patronized "naturally by rich people, not necessarily in the movie business—all kinds from all over" (p. 6). As in the Hollywood short stories, Fuchs is dealing with the very rich. Geographically and socially, he is now miles away from Williamsburg, but essentially things are not much changed. Underneath the wealthy facade, these people, too, are human and low.

The story is set just before the collapse of the studio system described in "The Golden West." It is the late 1950s, a time when studios are experiencing their final moments of power and when television is beginning to steal the audience from the movies. The studios' heyday is certainly over; now it is only a question of time.

To this hotel, at this time, comes Adele Hogue, box-office star and movie queen, who is on the verge of a mental breakdown. With her she brings three children, the wreckage of her life, and a new series of potentially juicy scandals for the gossip magazines and newspapers. Adele has escaped to this resort after bolting from the set of her latest movie. She has stalled the production of the film and has left the producers and executives in a frenzy, since her action may force the moneymen to halt production and cause the studio to lose millions of dollars already spent on the movie. In a desperate move, the talent agency that handles Adele Hogue sends Burt Claris, an agent who has dealt with her in the past, to Palm Springs to talk Adele into returning to the picture.

Claris is a "grifter" and a loser. A former college football star, he is now a leg man for a major talent agency. As a younger man, he was able to capitalize on his college success and athletic good looks to get into high society. He married the daughter of a very wealthy family and, through his father-in-law's connections, was able to land his present job. Claris' father-in-law got him the job mainly "so that he would have something to do and keep occupied," and he is considered mere "window dressing" at the agency. Besides the job, the family has provided Claris with servants, a large house, and "a nurse for the baby when the child came along."

Claris, however, is uncomfortable in the world of the rich; he doesn't really belong there. In this world he is a drifter with no sense of permanence. He does his "bogus, makeshift" job in a workmanlike way but is not very good at it. And he is equally inept as a husband and a father. Not very happy in his marriage, he is "consistently unfaithful to his young inexperienced wife." In fact one of his illicit liaisons has been with Adele Hogue, to whom he now must return and plunge himself into a difficult, sensitive situation that he is not competent to handle.

The Palm Springs resort to which Claris must travel is a West Coast version of Neptune Beach—the wasteland has now extended across the country. Unlike Neptune Beach, Palm Springs is not a place of violence, murder, or underworld activities, but it is a place of extreme moral decay. The theme of dissolution, the breakdown of substantive values, is explored throughout the story, most effectively in Fuchs's portrayal of the female guests at the hotel. They are "second and third wives of men who made big money in meat, oil, or textiles. The men had their offices in St. Louis, in Chicago, in cities in Texas, and since they or their wives insisted on living on the West Coast, they were constantly obliged to be in transit, commuting from point to point" (pp. 6–7). They are like a band of Furies, and Fuchs occasionally focuses his attention on them during the novel to enforce his exposé of Hollywood society. They lie in the sun and gossip, discussing hairdos and beauty operations; all of them have been "in the business at one time or another as stand-ins or stock girls." With men their feelings are "overwhelmingly tender and solicitous and at the same time impersonal, a kindness which they could discontinue seemingly without an instant's feeling or trace of remembrance." These are callous people leading jaded lives—normal relationships have been replaced by isolation and perversion.

Fuchs also uses the Los Angeles freeway, with its immense traffic tie-ups and noise, as a recurring symbol of what modern life has become. Industrialization, expansion, and modernization have all contributed to the process of dehumanizing, frustrating, and debilitating man. The freeway has also contributed to the laying waste of a land that was once beautiful, new, and promising. The final frontier has been perverted:

They had great jams on the freeways. Normally the traffic drummed ahead in its furor, the cars careening at sixty-five miles an hour or more over the four-lane sweep of the freeway; but when an accident occurred, a collision or breakdown, the cars piled up in a fearful chain reaction, slamming into one another and hurtling themselves all over the hard, concrete roadbed, blocking the four lanes, and then the traffic backed up for miles and the whole roaring maelstrom came to a halt. (p. 22)

Such descriptions reach deeper, clearly representing the stagnation of modern life, where everything is confused, tied up, and chaotic. Fuchs is here developing his own variation on the road as a metaphor in American fiction. In *Huckleberry Finn,* there was enough time and space to "light out for the territory," and even as late as the 1950s, Jack Kerouac's Dean Moriarty and his friends still enjoyed the prospect of lighting out "on the road" for Colorado. Fuchs's freeway suggests America's inability to move any farther. Here the road of escape has come to a dead end: all possibilities for change have been exhausted, and people can no longer even get from one place to another. The butterfly that was once incongruously confined in a subway car has now found a cage in the freeway.

The freeway is also a place of death. Early in the novel, Louis, the hotel steward, tells Claris that Pepi Straeger, an actor, has been killed in a freeway accident. Straeger in many ways resembled Claris: he too was a loser, a hanger-on whom Claris had once helped to get a bit part in a film. Recently, however, Straeger was having a stroke of good fortune, having persuaded a wealthy woman to marry him. Straeger's luck, however, ends abruptly on the freeway:

Straeger, as soon as he had connected solidly with the lady, had had his teeth newly recapped, that expert theatrical job they did for the top stars, and Claris thought of the caps, the vacuum-fired porcelain jacket crowns, strewn now somewhere on the concrete pavement of the highway. . . . (p. 39)

The themes of dissolution, superficiality, and the shattering of dreams, all prevalent in Hollywood fiction, are realized and given focus in these lines. The superficiality of Hollywood life is symbolized by the false teeth shattered and strewn all over the freeway, the symbol of modern Los Angeles. Straeger's own life, that of a failure, and the abrupt end to his soaring hopes make the Hollywood myth of instant success a lie. In Straeger's story, Claris should be able to see himself, and to a certain extent he does. Claris's story is also one of failure and opportunism, and though Claris will not die a physical death, the end of the novel will reveal that Hollywood has killed his soul.

The central presence of the novel, however, is Adele Hogue. All the main characters of the book move around her, and it is her decision that initiates the novel's action. However, Stanley Kauffmann's remark that Adele "seems an amalgam of Fuchs' experiences rather than a person"[29] points to a serious weakness in the character, which has appeared under other names in other books, on television, and in the movies. Hers is the rather tired exposé of the big Hollywood star's life deglamorized. Fuchs follows this familiar figure "behind the scenes," as others have done, and finds there, as usual, not a happy person content with her success, but a miserable, lonely, neurotic wreck of a human being. This formula is too predictable to command much interest anymore.

Adele is, like many characters in Hollywood fiction, two-dimensional, and yet there is something compelling about her, something achieved by the poetic and phantomlike quality of the whole work. John Updike writes that the book reads "as if Fuchs were groping through a dream that puzzles him, dazzles him."[30] The novel reads like a kind of reverie, and Adele, like a modern-day version of Dante's Francesca, seems to float tantalizingly before us, elusive, mysterious, fragile, and desirable:

She held her shoulders straight, carrying her body with that clear-striding, forthright, sexual quality they had and which they knew they had. It was the way they were put together; it was the bones in them. It was a readiness or acquiescence to use the body for all the pleasure it could give, a readiness they picked up from their mothers, in the Hollywood malt shops, out of the air.

If Adele's essential "human" characteristics chain her to earth, another part of her nature remains elusive, phantomlike. Fuchs himself seems awed by this indefinable aura of glamor, and his success in evoking it finally saves his heroine from mere stereotype. He does not try to analyze the mystery, but merely acknowledges the presence of a "force," an "energy" that distinguishes the movie star from less colorful mortals: " 'Star quality,' the executives in the front offices called it, using this term as a definition, a term which of course didn't explain anything" (p. 84). In an essay written the same year *West of the Rockies* was published, Fuchs elaborates on this phenomenon:

Over the years I wonder at times at the quality that exists in the main-eventers—whatever it is they have in them that makes them stars, whether they know they have it in them or whether they consciously work at it and build it up, whether they have anything in them at all.[31]

The mystery of stardom is directly related to the larger mystery of the motion picture itself. The formula for a successful picture also remains a mystery to Fuchs; somehow they were made, and somehow some of them became great hits:

No one knew. Wizardry was involved. The studio people with their unrelenting practicality, held solely with the instinct of the audience. . . . And yet the exasperating dilemma remained that what you were to give the audience was a quantity really indefinable, ephemeral, everlastingly elusive.[32]

The novel reflects this "elusiveness," which perhaps in part explains its lack of depth, for its central mystery is one of fluid, glittering surfaces that resist the paralysis of definition.

Adele's "human" side, however, firmly links her with the mediocre, commonplace, "low company" of the novel. Fuchs undercuts her at her first appearance, and then throughout the novel, he gradually reveals facts about her past which diminish her in the reader's eyes. When Claris first enters her room at the hotel, he observes:

She was ordinary, immature, smaller and slighter, as they all seemed off screen, altogether incapable of surmounting the difficulties that were besetting her. (p. 12)

Adele's physical appearance, her mental condition, and her skin disorders reflect the difficult and emotionally trying life that she has led. Her career as an actress has followed a Hollywood script formula, the typical overnight success story: "They had walked Adele in front of the cameras for four or five hundred feet of film—that was all it had been; she hadn't even had a line—and the walk, the four hundred feet of film had been enough."

Success was easy, but living with it has been very difficult. Late in the novel, she reveals to Claris some of the less savory moments of her wretched life, which have left her broken and permanently scarred. Adele discusses her first marriage and divorce; the man had been too old for her: "they all said she was looking for a father figure."

Two other events have had a profound effect on her: her abortion ("She spoke of the seedy business district in the daylight, the vacant room over the store in Santa Monica, the doctor saying to her, 'If you scream I'll throw you out into the street.' ") and her mother's death from cancer.[33] Her experiences have stripped her of defenses and also of illusions. She understands desperate people, for she has experienced nothingness. Her life has been an education in darkness, as well as an exercise in maintaining and living an illusion.

At present Adele is getting over the effects of another divorce. The psychological fallout from this latest disaster is primarily responsible for her present trouble. She has come to the Case Hotel because the Cases are the only friends she can think of, and because, as is soon revealed, Adele once had an affair with Harry Case, Fannie's ex-husband. Despite the fact that the affair broke up the Cases' marriage, and although Adele eventually backed out of marrying Harry Case, the three remain friends. Still, the relationship is a strange one, as Adele seems to take a kind of masochistic delight in seeing Harry and opening up old scars.

The portraits of Fannie and Harry Case are the best in the novel. Since the novel concentrates primarily on Adele, they do not appear often, but Fuchs's careful delineation of significant gestures and details makes them the book's most memorable characters.

Fannie is a "take-charge gal" who knows the ropes, having experienced the ups and downs of Hollywood life and now having achieved a secure position that she wants to keep. She is not cynical, but she knows that life is hard, and despite the difficulty that Adele and her husband have put her through, she still retains a sense of compassion and understanding. She is "the classic Hollywood first wife, the one discarded when the ambitious husband, finally hitting it big, goes after a younger woman."[34]

Fannie is concerned about the potential repercussions of a meeting between Adele and Harry, and she tries to convince her ex-husband to tread softly. Harry Case, who is "low slung, pugnacious with a prize fighter's stance and truculence,"[35] is an ex-racketeer whose shady business dealings have brought him success. Much like Papravel of *Summer in Williamsburg*, he is a fast-talking, conniving, mannerless man who is used to getting what he wants. Case came to California as a young man and worked his way up in the rackets. Socially ambitious, he liked to hang around the movie elite, and even now he yearns for their favors and likes to be seen in their company.

Despite the fact that he was spurned by Adele, Harry still feels great affection for her. As soon as the new trouble starts, he comes running to the hotel, expressing concern for her and her children and for the future of the movie. Fannie, however, knows him better than that. Despite the concern, she knows that he has deeper, more selfish motives:

Who are you trying to fool? . . . Don't I know you from the old days? You were star crazy then and you're still star crazy. You saw your chance and you came busting all over yourself. You can't wait to get your fingers on her. (p. 33)

The first confrontation of Harry and Adele is like a championship boxing match. Each knows the other's vulnerable spots, exactly where to strike. Before Adele, even Harry's physical appearance seems to change:

It was amazing how the pugnacity in him transformed him physically; without it he would be insignificant, would shrink back to size. (p. 47)

Harry understands Adele very well. He warns her that she is in danger:

Stupid, dumb broad. . . . You know and I know and the lamppost knows sooner or later you're going to fold, so what are you raising an unnecessary holler for? Nobody expects you to be the greatest superstar you think people think you have to be. Just go out there and wiggle your butt, that's all they want from you. . . . Just do what they tell you to do and you'll be all right. (pp. 50–51)

Adele counters with stories about Harry's past, about his constant attempts to be seen with movie stars. The dialogue here is crisp and sharp, effectively conveying the emotional conflicts within the central antagonists and within the two spectators, Fannie and Bert Claris.

During this scene it is revealed that Harry has promised the moneymen and producers that he will get Adele back on the picture, which infuriates Adele, for she doesn't want him to think that he can control her life. The argument also brings out details about Adele's latest marriage, to the son of an English duke, who turned out to be worthless. She married him for his title and position and because of a great desire to be socially respectable, to be thought an aristocrat. Harry reveals that Adele's English gentleman really had no money, "and was completely dependent on his father for support." The father, however, "was the tightwad of the century," and didn't give his son a penny. Adele had to foot all the bills herself. All the showy excursions through the posh European spots cost her four hundred thousand dollars, leaving her broke and depressed, and prompting the sudden withdrawal that has brought her to Fannie's again.

These scenes between Harry and Adele illustrate certain aspects of the theme of dissolution characteristic of the Hollywood novel: the loss or confusion of identity (Adele does not know who she is anymore, or even what kind of person she should be), the corruption of love and normal relationships (Adele's relationships with Harry and with her latest husband, and Fannie's relationship with Harry), the death of values and dreams, and the pervasive sense of the waste of human energy.

Adele's life has been a series of disasters, a waste of energy—"and it all goes on in a goldfish bowl." Harry is perceptive enough to understand this and to realize that her only salvation lies in the continuation of her career. He is also astute enough to see that the movie business as it is (the studio system) is crumbling and that movie producers no longer have the money or patience to put up with a temperamental star. The coddled movie queen is a vanishing breed, and Harry tries to persuade Adele to face reality: "The only time you know what's happening to you is when you're facing the cameras, and that's the one thing you have to run away from." Harry spares nothing in forcing Adele to confront the memory of past disasters and the prospect of those that lie ahead if she continues her headlong flight from herself.

Two other people occasionally figure in the action of the novel. Both are involved with the production and financing of Adele's film, but despite the crisis, neither of them seems really worried. They are too concerned with sex and with their own wrecked lives to worry about Adele or the picture. Their function in the novel is merely to reemphasize the debasement of the Hollywood life-style.

Robert Wigler, the producer, hangs around the hotel but takes no real active part in trying to help Claris. His concern hinges on the cost of the delay, "his sets standing idle in Culver City, the overhead mounting, and the actress here in Palm Springs, intransigent" (p. 23). Still, he is not really worried about it—Harry Case seems more concerned than he does. Wigler has grown too familiar with the Hollywood game to care much. The Hollywood novel's emphasis on resignation and cynicism is embodied in Wigler's character. Speaking to Claris, Wigler reveals his philosophy for dealing with actors and with life:

It seems they go out of their way intentionally looking for headaches. People are unhappy. . . . You want to know why? Simple. I'll tell you. Time passes. We wear out. Life disappoints us. Not only movie stars. Everyone. (p. 29)

This attitude has pervaded Fuchs's fiction since *Summer in Williamsburg.* Time has not changed his mind or altered his views—men still lead dull, uneventful lives, grow weary, become disappointed, and die. Perhaps life is a bit more colorful in Hollywood, but that is all.

Wigler himself is an unhappy man. He "had been unluckly straight down the line with women." He had a disastrous marriage (his wife turned out to be a prostitute) and attempted suicide. Now he is older, "without resources," and "he couldn't seem to daydream anymore, and this, too, disturbed him."

Dick Prescott, the head agency man who sent Claris to deal with Adele Hogue, is totally unconcerned with the case. He is a selfish man, ready to take any easy way out of any situation. Discussing the Hogue case with Prescott, Claris complains, "If anything goes wrong I'm the heavy"; Prescott replies, "Why should I jeopardize myself?"

It is all too plain that Bert Claris is getting help from nowhere. Wigler lacks the strength to really care, Prescott is uninterested, and Harry Case seems to be merely antagonizing Adele. These people do not respect Claris either. They know that he is not highly regarded at the agency, and, with the exception of Wigler, who uses him occasionally as a shoulder to cry on, nobody really pays any attention to him. There is good reason for this, for Claris is out of place in the fast-paced movie world, and even though he has had intimate relations with Adele, he doesn't really understand how to handle her, especially in a crisis.

Claris is also worried that this crisis may reveal his past with Adele, ruin his marriage, and destroy his easy life. He is smart enough, however, to realize that getting involved with Adele might be beneficial to his career. After a meeting with Prescott, he considers the possibility of cashing in on his relationship with Adele:

There were people who cashed in on actresses. Claris could think immediately of three or four names—men who had latched on, marrying them or living with them, who had set themselves up as producers, as figures to be reckoned with. (p. 78)

Such thoughts run through Claris's mind off and on through much of the novel, as he tries to decide what to do.

In despair he leaves Palm Springs and returns home, where he learns that his wife has been unfaithful to him for a long time and now wants a divorce. Dazed by this discovery, he goes to his lawyer to discuss custody of the child, but with ulterior motives: "he knew and the lawyer knew that what he was after was to use the child, the threat of a courtroom fight—to wheedle or blackmail a lump cash settlement out of the family" (p. 120). The lawyer tells him that the family can easily wipe him out if a court case should come up. The scene reeks of a kind of "lowness" that Fuchs finds so degrading. Later Claris finds out that, having lost his family connections, he has also lost his job with the agency.

Stripped of everything, he decides to return to Adele, aware that his only chance lies with her. He decides to propose himself as her agent: "Claris knew enough of the business to handle the studio details, to make deals and front for her. He could provide a genuine support and service . . ." (p. 127). He dreads discussing the arrangement with her, realizing how false and selfish such a deal would be, "she knowing and he knowing and both of them proceeding in the pretense of decency and good heart" (p. 138). But he manages to convince himself to do it anyway.

They decide to get married—Adele reaching once again for some stability, though she knows it probably won't work, and Claris desperate for this one chance. Fannie, who doesn't think much of the

idea, sums up Adele's attitude when she responds to Harry's query as
to who Claris actually is: "A man. What the hell. Another husband,
another marriage—marriage two hundred and twelve" (p. 157). For
Claris the marriage means status in the Hollywood community, for he
now will be a big independent agent. Announcing the engagement at
this time will also help Adele's career, for she has damaged her
reputation by leaving the set of her latest picture, and a new romance
will put her back in the limelight, back in demand: "That was why she
had to go through the announcement whether she was in the mood or
not . . ." (p. 163).

A press conference is called and the engagement is announced.
Fuchs's description is significant:

Adele smiled as he came up, and made room for him beside her. They stood
together, arm in arm. Transcending the ignominies that had passed between
them, falling into the guise they would now assiduously practice with each
other, they presented themselves to the onlookers, brazening it out,
challenging them and uncaring. (p. 165)

The book ends with this "guise," this arrangement, that will take the
place of any real solution to the problems that blight the lives of these
two. Neither is pledging human responsibility or commitment.
Claris's motives are selfish, and Adele, as her lips, "moving sound-
lessly," whisper "I love you, I love you" to Claris in front of the press
corps, is slipping once again into her world of unreality. She is once
again the actress doing the only thing she really knows how to do.

Thematically *West of the Rockies* resembles Fuchs's earlier fiction:
it is closest in theme and tone to *Low Company*. The themes of
dissolution and human decay are pervasive, and the Palm Springs
landscape is as much of a wasteland to Fuchs as Neptune Beach. The
people are still mediocre and low—they still commit abominations
and are guilty of "hardening of the heart."

Stylistically and structurally, however, the book represents an
important departure from the earlier fiction. In *West of the Rockies*
the plot structure is cinematic; indeed the story was originally
intended for the screen.[36] Fuchs proceeds by focusing on one
character, then almost dissolving him out of the frame to concentrate
on someone or something else. He is continually cross-cutting
between various locales (indoors and outdoors, the hotel and the
freeway). Certainly he used these techniques in his earlier novels,

but rarely within the same sequence. In the early novels, particularly *Summer in Williamsburg*, there were clear lines of demarcation between one scene and another. *West of the Rockies* exhibits more sophisticated eut-and-dissolve processes, as Fuchs moves back and forth between different characters and events that occur simultaneously. The narrative in this novel is also more "sensual than reflective"—the poetic and sense-oriented quality of its descriptions and of its evocations of the landscape represents a departure from the earlier fiction. Finally, Fuchs uses little dialogue in this novel, but summarizes thoughts and actions rather than dramatizing them. Here its likeness to a screen treatment is most evident, for the film director is expected to flesh out what Fuchs has merely sketched in. Perhaps this accounts, in part, for the weakness of this novel, for though Fuchs is capable of beautiful lyric passages, he is much more adept at writing dialogue and creating action.

Fuchs's experimentation with a new kind of structure and a different narrative style is not really new. Each of Fuchs's novels is different from the others—chronologically they may be labeled naturalistic, tragic-comic, symbolic, and lyrical. Yet the overriding themes and the central vision have remained intact. In 1937 Fuchs, referring to the inhabitants of Neptune Beach, wrote: "it was not enough to call them low and pass on." Daniel Fuchs did then "pass on," but after over thirty years in the Hollywood jungle he offers another look, and his vision has not changed: man is still "low" and the essence of life is still impossible for the artist to capture.

In his 1971 essay "Days in the Gardens of Hollywood," after describing his reactions upon first seeing the beautiful California landscape, he concludes by recording his reaction to a recent tremor in the Los Angeles area:

The earth staggers and rolls. Power lines go down; the sky flares up. There is an incredible tumult of noise—doors and windows slamming in their frames, books tumbling to the floor, the bricks of the chimneys smashing to the pavement of the driveway. It goes on and on and doesn't stop. All we can do that morning of the Ninth, is to stand there huddling in a helpless fright—and then I suddenly understand, stark and plain and unalterable. Mystery is explained: nothing is given freely, payment is exacted.

For the boon of the work, for the joy of leisure, the happy lazy days; for the castles and drowsy back-lots; for the stalwarts I've come to know, John and Bob and Sam; for the parties at Barney's, the times at Phil's; the flowers, the sycamores, the blessings of the sun.[37]

Nothing is freely given. Dues must always be paid. Perhaps this is a hint that the final judgment is soon at hand: man has now crossed a continent—the new world has been explored and exploited from coast to coast. . . .

CHAPTER 6

A Gathering of Stories

MOST of Daniel Fuchs's short stories are uncollected, to be found only in back issues of various magazines. Only a few have been published in book form: three appear in a volume which also includes short stories by Jean Stafford, William Maxwell, and John Cheever,[1] some have appeared in O. Henry Prize–winning anthologies, and a number in other collections such as *The Best Short Stories from the New Yorker*. Many of his best pieces (including the essays), however, have never been anthologized or collected, which is unfortunate, for some of these pieces are excellent in themselves and for the light they shed on the fiction.

The stories, mostly formula pieces designed for a wide audience, appeared in such mass circulation magazines as *Collier's* and *Saturday Evening Post*. The plots are exciting: usually a hero or heroine becomes involved in a situation in which success or ruin is imminent. Action proceeds through quick twists of fortune. There are indications that all will be lost, but usually fortune favors the protagonist and everything turns out well. Fuchs admits that the editorial policy of the magazines dictated the form of these stories:

Capt. Brandt, editor at the *Saturday Evening Post* once told me the definition of a short story ending is a resolution "which gives the reader the fullest satisfaction." That's why the *Collier's* stories ended as they did.[2]

Readable and entertaining, these stories give some notion of what made a successful screenwriter for Hollywood studios.

The stories Fuchs wrote for the *New Yorker*, however, represent his finest achievements as a short-story writer. They are brief "slice of life" sketches, dealing for the most part with poor people in New York City tenements, those people whose lives Fuchs explored with such affection and honesty in the early novels. Life here is squalid, petty, and harsh; people are just people, with nothing grand or noble about

143

them. They are shown making awkward attempts at love and communication, as most of these stories deal with love, or man's failure at love, the limitations of the flesh, and man's inability to rise above the earth.

In these stories Fuchs is not interested in presenting an action, but in dramatizing a condition. He is concerned with showing life as it is, and, as he makes clear in *Summer in Williamsburg*, life (unlike most dramatic or narrative art) has no real drama. In these stories Fuchs creates situations which reveal the private struggle that each individual undergoes inside himself every day in the random, seemingly meaningless and undramatic events of the common routine.

The story "People on a Planet"[3] provides a useful introduction to this nondramatic technique. Merely a slice of life, this story has no real action or plot. A plane carrying a group of passengers across America is grounded in Salt Lake City because of the weather. Fuchs concentrates his attention on a number of the passengers, all of whom are locked up within themselves, concerned only with their particular problems. One couple is having difficulties with their marriage; an English couple is concerned about missing a boat called *The China Clipper*, which is due to leave California; some of the officers in the control tower are having problems trying to land another plane because of the fog. Nothing else happens. The story ends before the fog lifts, so the outcomes of the various dilemmas are never revealed. Fuchs has just portrayed people being themselves in an airport for a short period of time: they scurry about; they have difficulty communicating with others; they seem to be helpless before circumstance. The futility of man's activity on earth is revealed in moments like these.

Fuchs utilizes the same kind of technique in "Crap Game."[4] The setting is a New York City subway station platform, where a number of men are shooting craps. The game is quiet and peaceful until a woman begins to complain about gambling in a public place. This infuriates one of the men named McCarty (clearly related to the gambler Moe Karty in *Low Company*, who shares McCarty's hot temper—both *Low Company* and "Crap Game" were published in 1937), who tells her to mind her own business. Outraged, the woman goes off to get a policeman.

During her absence McCarty addresses the people on the platform in an attempt to justify his reaction. A number of people answer, saying that they agree that gambling is wrong in a public place, which further infuriates McCarty. A minister intercedes, but McCarty is disrespectful and walks away. Eventually the train comes, a number of people get on, and the story ends. The story again has pictured an ordinary occurrence, part of an average day for the average New Yorker.

While many of the stories retain this basic structure, most of them deal with specific themes, particularly human isolation. "The Apathetic Bookie Joint"[5] is a poignant picture of a man's dashed hopes, a reminder that life usually does not deliver what one hopes and yearns for. Barlow is a sensitive man caught up in an insensitive world. A graduate public accountant who failed the CPA exam, he now operates a bookie stand for his brother-in-law. He dislikes the kind of life he leads and the people he is forced to deal with, but he endures. To add to his *tzuris*, Barlow is funny-looking and bald, and people tease him because of this. The story concentrates on details that reveal the physcial limitations of the flesh: the bartender (the bookie joint is in a bar) has bad feet; Buster, Barlow's assistant, has a sick stomach; and a "languid lady" who sits quietly at a table during the course of the story is suffering from a broken heart.

The story is told by an "I" narrator (possibly Fuchs), and a good portion of the story is devoted to Barlow's talking to the narrator:

You're a decent American boy. You've got understanding, you've got feeling. I can tell. You're a human being. . . . We could hold intellectual conversations together. . . . I'm a professional too you know."

The term "human being," the dominant motif in the story, operates on two levels. To be human is to be subject to limitations (physical ailments, disappointments), but it is also to be potentially good, capable of achieving more than a world of bookie joints and crap games might imply. To be human is to be able to do the proper and decent thing and to live with dignity in undignified surroundings.

The story ends with the intrusion of a policeman who has come to investigate the bookie joint. Barlow objects and the policeman teases and humiliates him (the incident is reminiscent of a gangster's treatment of Shorty in *Low Company*). Barlow begins to cry and runs out of the room yelling, "I don't care if I live or die." No one moves to help him. Man remains petty and low, and in such a world the sensitive man is bound to suffer.

The theme of lonely isolation touched on in the story of Barlow is expanded by Fuchs in a number of the later stories. "The Morose Policeman"[6] deals with Patrolman Jellicoe, a policeman whom the "I" narrator meets while serving as a literacy examiner at a Brooklyn school. Jellicoe is having troubles with his wife, an attractive woman who outwardly maintains a cordial relationship with her husband. But her commitment to the Communist party is straining their relationship. Jellicoe is made to feel self-conscious for being a policeman, and, as he readily admits, he hates "reds": "He hated them like poison, . . . up and down, crosswise, lengthwise and slantwise." Communication between man and wife is becoming impossible, and Jellicoe is "morose." There is love, but neither Jellicoe nor his wife knows how to make it work against the divisive effect of politics—people always seem to find some way of destroying the one good thing they have.

The story ends with Jellicoe revealing to the narrator the one pleasure he has in life, the joy of being alone in the shower:

Boy, I stand there for hours and hours, just soaking in the water. . . . I lose myself. I'm all closed up and shut away from the world—no worries, no grief, no nothing.

"A Clean Quiet House"[7] once again utilizes Fuchs's favorite image—"the butterfly in the subway." Charlie Coopersmith, riding the subway home, observes it:

The butterfly jerked in nervous curves over the heads of the passengers, and Charlie, smiling at the sight, twisted his head to watch it. That was how he came to notice Howard Hayman.

Charlie is excited about meeting Howard (Hayman is of course the name of the protagonist in *Summer in Williamsburg,* the first Fuchs character to see a butterfly on the subway), a former high-school classmate whom he hasn't seen in years. He invites him to his home to meet his wife and son.

When they arrive at Charlie's apartment, they discover that Mrs. Coopersmith is not home, so they sit and talk. Charlie goes to the refrigerator to get some food and discovers that it is packed with all kinds of meats and *hors d'oeuvres.* He is very pleased, for he is anxious to prove to Howard that his wife is an excellent homemaker. They prepare sandwiches, and then, too late, they discover a note from Mrs. Coopersmith:

Darling:
  Out getting manicure—baby with me. . . . Please don't upset party food
or upset anything. Darling, please be a good boy today. . . .

Charlie shrugs this off, and while eating they reminisce and laugh
about old times. After singing their old high-school alma mater,
Howard reflects:

Here we were—happy-go-lucky kids with all kinds of hopes and ambitions
and plans and a spark of life in us. What happened to us all? What have we
attained in the passage of the years? Not very much.

And Charles adds: "Include me, too. I'm a failure. I guess we're all
failures."
  Dreams do not come true, hopes remain unfulfilled, and happiness
is an emotion only associated with childhood. When Charlie's
wife comes home, she is angry at him for upsetting the house and her
food platters. The "happy marriage" with which he wanted to impress
Howard is exposed as a sham. The story closes with Charlie playing
children's games with his son. Retreating from reality in this way, like
Patrolman Jellicoe's taking a shower, is his only means of gaining
peace and momentary happiness.
  "Man in the Middle of the Ocean,"[8] one of Fuchs's longest stories,
also deals with a man's isolation from family and community. Arnold
Darcy, a civil engineer, works for the city as a building-plans
examiner. He seems to live a rather ordinary life, though, unlike
many of Fuchs's New York City protagonists, he is not poor. His
home life is not very happy, but Darcy goes through the motions to
preserve a tolerable atmosphere, "because the pediatrician advised it
for the sake of their son, to create a solid family atmosphere."
  The story centers on a conflict between Darcy and two of his
business colleagues. A large and wealthy corporation is willing to pay
off Darcy and his partners to overlook certain safety regulations in an
office building they are putting up. The partners are willing to do it,
but not Darcy. The story alternates between the pressure of the
uncomfortable situation at the office and the strained atmosphere at
home. Finally, one day he decides to leave home and office and move
into a hotel; the decision fills him with a sense of relief and freedom:

Darcy was tired of being helpless and uncertain all the time, flopping around
like a man drowning in the middle of the ocean. Darcy was tired of meanness.

After four relaxing days in the hotel room, he returns. The situation at the office has calmed down, and at home his wife is very quiet, "just neutral." During dinner, she slips him a note which expresses her shock at his action and seeks a promise that he will never repeat it. The note makes Darcy realize that he is again a "man in the middle of the ocean" doomed to be swallowed up once more into the desperate rhythm of office and home.

"The Man from Mars"[9] carries the desperation felt by Darcy slightly further. Mr. Bluestone, a retired businessman who is now living the "good life" in Florida with his children, has become very quiet and morose of late. His son remarks on this: "In your old age you suddenly become a regular Schopenhauer. . . . You're a philosopher. To you everything stinks."

The story takes place at a race track, where the Bluestones have gone to have a good time. Only Mr. Bluestone is not enjoying himself:

"A squirrel cage," he said. "Look at them. They laugh and cry. They get happy, they feel bad. They're all excited. But what does it all mean? What does it all add up to? A squirrel cage, yes."

The squirrel cage recalls the restriction of the butterfly on the subway. Mr. Bluestone, with his new perspective, sees life as a prison. Fuchs alternates between Mr. Bluestone's wry comments and the excitement his children feel, accentuating the contrast between the joy of the young and the cynicism of the old man. Every time the children place a bet, a man named Willy calls them "suckers." Bluestone, like old Miller in *Summer in Williamsburg*, sees life as a series of frenetic activities which lead nowhere, a process inexplicable and ephemeral. As Bluestone's son announces that he has lost his bet, Willie comes running by, shouting: "Suckers! You've been roped in!" This prompts Johnny (Mr. Bluestone's son) to ask:

"Who does he think he is. . . . The Messiah?"
"Who knows?" Mr. Bluestone asked mournfully. "Who can tell? Why not?"

Life is a joke, a game which man is suckered into playing but which he cannot hope to win. "The Man from Mars" is certainly Fuchs's most pessimistic story.

"The First Smell of Spring, and Brooklyn,"[10] one of Fuchs's most beautiful pieces, is a short tale about hopes unfulfilled. It is a simple tale, but artistically handled. The "I" narrator wakes up to discover that spring has finally arrived. When he goes outside his apartment to get his bottle of milk, he discovers a note:

Dear Friend,
 Do you, too, find life tedious and uninviting at times? I wonder whether you would be interested in a rendezvous purely along Platonic lines. If so, you will find me waiting at Dineen's. . . .

The narrator, who seems bored and somewhat lonesome, is taken by the note. It offers the promise of adventure or romance, or at least something new and exciting.

He goes to Dineen's and waits, sitting in a booth behind a couple having a fight. Most of the story is taken up by the narrator's waiting and the couple's fighting. During this time the narrator reflects:

So there I was, waiting for nothing in the bar. For company I had an unhappy, quarrelling couple, a bartender and some waiters who kept reserved within their private concerns whatever they were, and a bookmaker's clerk who was sadly absorbed in his glass of beer and the rosy dreams of youth. And it was spring again.

No one comes to meet him; nothing happens; there is no real promise. Winter turns into spring, but nothing changes. On his way home the narrator meets Gloria, a high-school student who lives in the building. It turns out that it was she who sent the note. Slightly disgusted, the narrator returns to his building, back to the noise and activity that characterize life in Brooklyn.

There are two other prominent themes in the stories (both important in the first two novels), and all the remaining pieces feature one or the other of them. The first of these themes is the death of romantic love. In the first two novels, marriage is determined by women on the basis of economic stability. In *Summer in Williamsburg* Tessie marries Schlausser, whom she doesn't love, rather than Philip, whom she does, because Schlausser is established in business and makes a good living, while Philip is still a college boy with no real prospects. In the world Fuchs depicts, a world where the sole business of life is getting up to make a living "so that tomorrow they would be able to make a living another day," marriage becomes an economic consideration, not a romantic one.

"Love in Brooklyn"[11] develops this theme, presenting, as the title suggests, a portrait of what "love" means in the Brooklyn of the 1930s.

The "I" narrator in the story habitually waits in the park to meet a girl named Gertrude at a specific time when she walks with two of her friends. The narrator and Gertrude enjoy each other's company because they have common intellectual interests, such as Joyce and Proust. Gertrude's friend Ruth, however, persuades her that it is more important to pursue a man with prospects. (By the end of the story, Ruth succeeds in getting herself engaged to a doctor.) Under her influence, Gertrude decides to be more practical, and stops seeing the narrator. She changes her attitude about dating and her appearance; even her walk takes on a new kind of swagger. The last time they see each other, Gertrude explains her new manner (and the philosophy of her society) to the narrator: ". . . When all's said and done it boils down to this: at bottom every girl wants a husband. I can't continue fooling myself indefinitely."

"There's Always Honolulu"[12] is a story that deals with the realities of love, its lack of romance, and its place in the cycle of human existence. The story takes place during yet another hot and sticky New York City summer, when the people like to sit on apartment roofs hoping for a breeze. Martin Beckett refuses to go up to his roof because he knows Marion, his steady girl friend, will be there and he doesn't want to see her because he has heard that she is planning to go away to the coast of Maine for a few days with a Mr. Charney; he is jealous and angry. He finally does go up to the roof, however, where he sees her and tells her that he has always hoped to marry her. Marion is moved and tells Martin that the story about going to Maine was just a story to impress her girl friends. Actually she is going to Rockaway to help her married sister with the kids. This is reality: not Maine or Puerto Rico, but just Brooklyn and the only kind of romance to be found in Brooklyn.

Mr. Pavel, an old man who has been observing the young couple, comments:

Only, here right in front of my eyes I watch two kids. They play around. They grow up. Suddenly they're mature adults and they blossom out into a full fledged love affair. You can't change human nature, of course, but every time it happens I like to look on and watch it. It's beautiful, I suppose.

The "I suppose" is ironic, for Pavel realizes that there is really little beauty to the cycle he is describing. Soon the "love affair" will end and the continuous drudgery of everyday life will replace it, permanently.

Stories which deal with the theme of trying to "dream a way out of Williamsburg" comprise the second thematic group. The central characters of these stories are descendants of Cohen and Max Balkan, dreamers who, dissatisfied with their dingy lives, attempt to exist in a world of dreams and romance, a world that bears no relationship to the real one.

The best of these stories is "The Amazing Mystery at Storick, Dorschi, Pflaumer, Inc.,"[13] which deals with George Pattinger, an office worker in the collection department of Storick, Dorschi, Pflaumer, Inc. He is bald, awkward, and unnoticed by the women in the department: "He might have been an article of furniture for all they noticed him." Pattinger is in love with an office girl named Mildred Mosser, who of course refuses to take him seriously. To gain some sort of revenge on the office girls, Pattinger decides to take a cross-country flight during which he sends back to the office post-cards from various parts of the country. He is sure that the women will be impressed by his travels and that he will gain respect in their eyes as a man of the world.

While on the plane he gets an opportunity to act out his fantasies. To one woman sitting next to him, he affects an English accent and pretends that he is a famous international correspondent. Later he tells a stewardess that he is James Joyce. A reporter from a Salt Lake City newspaper overhears him and, believing that Pattinger is Joyce, takes his picture for the paper. When Pattinger returns to New York, however, the experience no longer seems worthwhile. He fears the prospect of explaining to his mother that he has spent all of his savings, and then he learns that he has been fired from his job for missing work. Pattinger is left with nothing—no job and no money. He has succeeded in intriguing the office girls, particularly Mildred, but it no longer really matters. Pattinger leaves his office in a despondent frame of mind, having learned that reality is too powerful a force to contend with.

"A Girl Like Cele"[14] and "Okay, Mr. Pappendas, Okay"[15] also deal with this theme. Cele is a Brooklyn girl who would rather be involved in the glamorous social world of the East Side of Manhattan. She treats her friends and current boyfriend, Philip, indifferently because they don't share her dreams, nor do they treat her as she would like to be treated. Her attitude infuriates her friends; one of them, Millicent, gets right to the heart of Cele's problem when she says:

Your head is filled with all these wonderful illusions of Park Avenue. . . .

They're wonderful illusions—we all have them; but they're not real. They're
not for us. We live in Brooklyn, you know. They're nothing substantial when
you have to live day by day.

Cele is considering having a relationship with John Starbuck, a
native of Oregon, whom she met during the summer. Starbuck
conceives of all New Yorkers as glamorous people, and it is this
attitude above all that Cele finds irresistible. At the story's end Cele is
left with nothing but her illusions; her attempts to be more than she is
have caused her to lose both Starbuck and Philip. Unlike most of
Fuchs's dreamers, however, Cele is not crushed by reality. She is
firm in her resolve to go on living her unreal life.

"Okay, Mr. Pappendas, Okay" is also set in Brooklyn. With a tone
as light as that of *Homage to Blenholt,* it centers on Howard, a barber
in Mr. Pappendas's barber shop, who dreams of being a movie writer.
He has already sent in a story idea about Mickey Mouse to the Disney
studios. It is a rather ridiculous story; Howard will obviously never
rise above the barbershop:

> . . . this idea . . . was to make Mickey Mouse a barber. So Donald Duck
> comes in for a shave. Get it? So this is one of those barber shops down in the
> basement with the windows high up. So a girl comes walking outside and she
> has to wait for a guy or something. So Mickey looks out and sees her legs. Get
> it? So he's just putting a hot towel on Donald Duck's face. . . .

Howard has decided not to tell anyone, except Mr. Pappendas, about
his idea because, like Max Balkan (whom he very much resembles),
he is tired of being teased about his schemes. When he gets an angry
note from his girl friend Terry, in which she mentions the movie idea,
he is puzzled. (Terry indicates that a friend of hers on the Coast read
about it in the trade reports.) He thinks that perhaps Disney has
taken his idea. Howard is excited; it seems that he has finally made it.
But again, Fuchsian reality deflates the dream, as it is revealed that
the letter was just a joke devised by Terry and the manicurist at the
barber shop, who overheard Howard telling Mr. Pappendas about
the idea. The story, like *Homage to Blenholt,* ends on a sad note.
Howard is embarrassed and crushed, unable to accept Mr. Pappendas's attempts to comfort him by renewing his hopes. The abrupt
encounter with reality, as usual in Fuchs, has destroyed the vitality
and the charm of the dream.

Thus a brief summary of the themes and plots of Fuchs's short pieces reveals a number of exquisite vignettes—beautiful, sad, accurate pictures of life. Further demonstrating the range of his versatility and talent, they complement nicely his considerable achievement as a novelist.

I *Summation*

Too often Daniel Fuchs's work has been dismissed with critical commonplaces: having written only four novels, he seems to lack the quality Anthony Burgess calls "bigness." Worse, he is accused of selling out to that malicious force "Hollywood," of turning out, instead of a weighty list of writings, a mere handful of B movies. However, when quality rather than quantity may be considered the measure of merit, then Fuchs's reputation will rest firmly on the strength of the three novels he wrote in the 1930s, which remain his most significant work as a writer of fiction.

The Williamsburg novels are extremely rich in detailing a way of life and presenting a sense of place. The characters are beautifully drawn, even the minor figures demonstrating a degree of individuality that is rare in fiction. The themes are complex and varied, having been developed and brought into sharp focus over the years.

Fuchs's most prevalent theme is entrapment. His characters live in a world from which there is no exit, populating (like their author) a universe that is limited to Williamsburg and the slum; there seems to be no other world beyond the confines of a few city blocks. Fuchs's world also seems to exist in a limbo, outside the dimension of time: days pass, but the past is only vaguely available, and the future is inaccessible. The present is all that matters.

Fuchs should not be dismissed, as he sometimes has been, as merely an interesting regional writer, a local colorist. His regional flavor is no more a limitation than that of Faulkner, Hawthorne, O'Hara, or the best of Sinclair Lewis (and it is not overstatement to put Fuchs's name in this company). Though firmly rooted in the Williamsburg milieu, Fuchs's themes and vision expand to universal significance, and his talent demands wider attention.

The themes of escape and entrapment which dominate *Summer in Williamsburg*, the dilemmas faced by young Philip Hayman in struggling to understand his world, are real and urgent. The novel has an immense scope, and in its attention to detail and character captures better than any other novel the world of the immigrant Jew in America.

Homage to Blenholt, tighter in structure than its predecessor, is also lighter in tone. More indebted to the novel of manners than to the realistic novel, Fuchs displays in this book a gift for "exuberant comedy,"[16] also influenced by the silent comedies of Harold Lloyd, Buster Keaton, and Charlie Chaplin. The Keaton characters' misadventures in the world of things, Chaplin's comedy of pathos, and Lloyd's brash, success-driven adventures are all given shape in this novel. Ultimately, however, Fuchs is closer in vision here to Chekhov in his mingling of the comic and the tragic: while he shows a firm hand in creating comedy—"the work of a young man enraptured by the discovery of his mimetic powers"[17]—the novel ultimately reflects Fuchs's sadness, a kind of gentle despair.

Low Company discards the comic tone, the questioning and earnest young men, the defeated but pure fathers, and instead presents a revised vision that is biting and bitter. Now Fuchs projects his themes in a nightmare world populated by grotesques, the kind of world that Yeats described as a prelude to "The Second Coming." Fuchs's powers to create characters and setting, and his increasing control of the novelistic form, have here attained complete mastery. As a portrait of a world on the verge of collapse, the mingling of the surreal with the real, the nightmare with the waking state, it is unsurpassed in American fiction; only West's *The Day of the Locust* can approach it.

Little of Fuchs's remaining work compares to these early novels, his shorter pieces being too limited in scope for a talent that needed the vast canvas of the novel. Recently, however, there have been signs of his regaining the earlier power: the later Hollywood essays (including "The Silents Spoke to the Immigrants") and parts of *West of the Rockies,* though different in style and technique from the earlier fiction, possess their own magic. Seemingly written in a dream state, they glide back and forth in time, evoking vivid images of scene and character and employing a poetic language with a force of its own to move the reader from passage to passage, from Williamsburg to Hollywood and back again. This new style is once again evident in his most recent story, "Ivanov's 'The Adventures of a Fakir' " (1975), and perhaps will culminate in the novel he is now writing.

To the page-counters Daniel Fuchs's output may seem small, even insignificant, but those who have read without counting—among them Irving Howe, Leslie Fiedler, Alfred Kazin, Howard Moss, Harvey Swados, John Updike, James T. Farrell, Mordecai Richler, and Irwin Shaw—have found Fuchs's work rich, complex, satisfying, and at times brilliant. His best work certainly deserves a place in the forefront of American literature. It is time that more critics and scholars read it and evaluated it and anthologized it. It will not be found wanting.

Notes and References

Chapter One

1. Fuchs in an interview with G. Miller, August 1, 1975.
2. Ronald Sanders, *The Downtown Jews* (New York, 1969), p. 5.
3. Michael Gold, *Jews Without Money* (1930; rpt. New York, 1972), p. 5.
4. Interview, August 1, 1975.
5. Daniel Fuchs, "The Silents Spoke to the Immigrants," *New York Times*, October 17, 1971, p. 13.
6. Interview, August 1, 1975.
7. Letter from Fuchs to G. Miller, December 9, 1975.
8. Daniel Fuchs, "Where Al Capone Grew Up," *New Republic*, September 9, 1931, p. 95.
9. Fuchs to Miller, December 9, 1975.
10. "The Silents Spoke to the Immigrants," p. 13.
11. Ibid.
12. Ibid.
13. Ibid.
14. Fuchs to G. Miller, December 9, 1975.
15. Letter from Fuchs to G. Miller, September 14, 1974.
16. Interview, August 1, 1975.
17. Ibid.
18. Ibid.
19. Ibid.
20. From Fuchs's Introduction to *3 Novels by Daniel Fuchs* (New York, 1961), v.
21. Interview, August 1, 1975.
22. Stanley Young, review of *Homage to Blenholt*, *New York Times*, February 23, 1936, p. 6.
23. Introduction to *3 Novels by Daniel Fuchs*, vii.
24. Ibid.
25. Interview, August 1, 1975.
26. Daniel Fuchs, "Writing for the Movies," *Commentary*, February 1962. This incident is also related in Joseph Blotner, *Faulkner: A Biography* (New York, 1974), p. 1133.
27. Letter from Fuchs to G. Miller, September 14, 1974.
28. Leonard Kriegel, *Edmund Wilson* (Carbondale, 1971), p. 16.
29. Edmund Wilson, *Axel's Castle* (1931; rpt. New York, 1969), p. 287.

30. Richard Pells, *Radical Visions and American Dreams* (New York, 1973), p. 159.

31. Granville Hicks, *The Great Tradition* (1933; rpt. Chicago, 1969), p. 304.

32. Michael Folsom, ed., *Mike Gold: A Literary Anthology* (New York, 1972), p. 206.

33. Quoted in Walter B. Rideout, *The Radical Novel in the United States* (1956; rpt. New York, 1966), p. 168.

34. Daniel Fuchs, *Summer in Williamsburg*, in *3 Novels by Daniel Fuchs* (New York, 1961), p. 314.

35. *Summer in Williamsburg*, p. 380.

36. David Madden, introduction to *Proletarian Writers of the Thirties* (Carbondale, 1968), xxx.

37. Walter Allen, *The Modern Novel* (New York, 1965), p. 176.

38. Pells, p. 184.

39. Allen Tate, "Three Types of Poetry," in *The Collected Essays* (Denver, 1959), p. 113.

40. Albert Halper, review of *Low Company*, *New Republic*, February 24, 1937.

41. For additional information on the *Forward* see Ronald Sanders, *The Downtown Jews*.

42. Allen Guttmann, *The Jewish Writer in America* (New York, 1971), p. 45.

43. John J. Clayton, *Saul Bellow: In Defense of Man* (1968; rpt. Bloomington, 1971), p. 31.

44. Quoted in the introduction of Irving Howe and Eliezer Greenberg, eds., *A Treasury of Yiddish Stories* (1954; rpt. New York, 1973), p. 51.

45. Daniel Fuchs, *Low Company* in *3 Novels by Daniel Fuchs* (New York, 1961), p. 311.

46. Harold Strauss, review of *Low Company*, *New York Times*, February 28, 1937, p. 6.

47. Howe and Greenberg, p. 9.

48. Maurice Samuel, *The World of Sholom Aleichem* (1943; rpt. New York, 1969), p. 16.

49. Howe and Greenberg, p. 55.

50. Howard Moss, "Daniel Fuchs: Homage to the Thirties," in *Writing Against Time* (New York, 1969), pp. 32–33.

51. Howe and Greenberg, p. 26.

52. Ruth R. Wisse, *The Schlemiel as Modern Hero* (Chicago, 1971), p. 3.

53. Daniel Fuchs, *Homage to Blenholt* in *3 Novels by Daniel Fuchs* (New York, 1961), p. 74.

54. Wisse, p. 53.

55. Howe and Greenberg, p. 40.

56. Ibid.

57. For further biographical information on West see Jay Martin, *Nathanael West: The Art of His Life* (New York, 1970).

58. Max F. Schulz, *Radical Sophistication* (Ohio, 1969), p. 36.

59. Victor Comerchero, *Nathanael West: The Ironic Prophet* (1964; rpt. Seattle, 1967), p. 13.

60. Nathanael West, *Miss Lonelyhearts* and *The Day of the Locust* (1933 and 1939; rpt. New York, 1962), p. 177.

61. Randall Reid, *The Fiction of Nathanael West* (Chicago, 1971), p. 157.

62. *Summer in Williamsburg*, p. 261.

63. Norman Podhoretz, "Nathanael West: A Particular Kind of Joking," in *Nathanael West: A Collection of Critical Essays*, ed. Jay Martin (Englewood Cliffs, N.J., 1971), p. 155.

64. *The Day of the Locust*, p. 61.

Chapter Two

1. Daniel Fuchs, *Summer in Williamsburg*, in *3 Novels by Daniel Fuchs* (New York, 1961), pp. 11–12. All further references to the novel are cited in the text and refer to this edition. The paperback edition, entitled *The Williamsburg Trilogy* (New York, 1972), uses the same pagination.

2. Ben Siegel, "FUCHS, Daniel," in *Contemporary Novelists*, ed. James Vinson (New York, 1972), p. 436.

3. Irving Howe, "Daniel Fuchs: Escape from Williamsburg," *Commentary*, July, 1948, p. 33.

4. Howard Moss, "Daniel Fuchs: Homage to the Thirties," in *Writing Against Time* (New York, 1969), p. 34.

5. Fuchs, Introduction to *3 Novels by Daniel Fuchs*, vi–vii.

6. Vernon Louis Parrington, *The Beginnings of Critical Realism in America: 1860–1920* (1930; rpt. New York, 1958), p. 323.

7. Stephen Crane, poem 96 of Uncollected Poems, in Joseph Katz, ed., *The Complete Poems of Stephen Crane* (Ithaca, 1972), p. 102.

8. Parrington, p. 324.

9. See also the relationship between Tommy Wilhelm and Dr. Tamkin in Saul Bellow's *Seize the Day*.

10. Hyatt Waggoner, *American Poets* (rpt. New York, 1968), p. 262.

11. Ralph Waldo Emerson, "The Over-Soul," in Irwin Edman, ed., *Emerson's Essays* (New York, 1951), p. 193.

12. See, for example, Jack Conroy's *The Disinherited*.

13. Isaac Bashevis Singer, *Gimpel the Fool and Other Stories* (1954; rpt. New York, 1969), p. 22.

14. Ben Siegel, *Isaac Bashevis Singer* (Minneapolis, 1969), p. 19.

15. Quoted in Charles Madison, *Yiddish Literature: Its Scope and Major Writers* (1968; rpt. New York, 1971), p. 93.

16. Humphrey Cobb, *Paths of Glory* (1935; rpt. New York, 1973), p. 202.

17. Sam Bluefarb, *The Escape Motif in the American Novel* (Columbus, 1972), p. 3.

18. West, pp. 2–3.

19. Howe, p. 30.

20. Hyatt Waggoner, Introduction to *The House of Seven Gables* (Boston, 1964), xxii.

Chapter Three

1. Irving Howe, "Daniel Fuchs: Escape from Williamsburg," *Commentary,* July 1948, p. 31.

2. Irving Howe, "Daniel Fuchs' Williamsburg Triology," in David Madden ed., *Proletarian Writers of the Thirties* (Carbondale, 1968), pp. 100–101.

3. George Meredith, "An Essay on Comedy," in Wylie Sypher, ed., *Comedy* (New York, 1956), p. 47.

4. Sypher, p. 193.

5. Ibid., p. 195.

6. A. Shaftymov, "Principles of Structure in Chekhov's Plays," in Robert L. Jackson, ed., *Chekhov: A Collection of Critical Essays* (Engelwood Cliffs, 1967), p. 84.

7. Daniel Fuchs, *Homage to Blenholt*, in *3 Novels by Daniel Fuchs* (New York, 1961), p. 77. All further references to the novel are cited in the text and refer to this edition.

8. Howe, "Escape from Williamsburg," p. 31.

9. Fyodor Dostoevsky, *Notes From Underground,* transl. Ralph Matlaw (New York, 1960), p. 3.

10. Dostoevsky, p. 25.

11. Ibid., p. 28.

12. Edward Wasiolek, *Dostoevsky: The Major Fiction* (Cambridge, 1964), p. 42.

13. Dostoevsky, pp. 49–50.

14. Ibid., p. 49.

15. Jan Kott, *Shakespeare Our Contemporary* (New York, 1966), p. 138.

16. It is interesting to note that Samuel Beckett, an admirer of Chaplin, uses a similar description to describe the gait of Watt:

> Watt's way of advancing due east, for example, was to turn his bust as far as possible towards the north and at the same time to fling out his right leg as far as possible to the south, and then to turn his bust as far as possible toward the south and at the same time to fling out his left leg as far as possible toward the north. . . . (p. 30, Evergreen edition)

17. Robert Payne, "Charlie Chaplin: Portrait of the Moralist," in Daniel Talbot, ed., *Film: An Anthology* (Los Angeles, 1969), p. 365.

18. Howe, "Daniel Fuchs: Escape from Williamsburg," p. 32.

Chapter Four

(Note: "Children of the Cold Sun" refers to a poem by David Wolff)

1. Irving Howe, "Daniel Fuchs: Escape from Williamsburg," *Commentary*, July 1948, p. 31.

2. Howard Moss, "Daniel Fuchs: Homage to the Thirties," in *Writing Against Time* (New York, 1969), p. 41.

3. Harold Strauss, review of *Low Company*, *New York Times*, February 28, 1937, p. 6.

4. James T. Farrell, review of *Low Company*, *Nation*, 144 (February 27, 1937), p. 244.

5. I am indebted here to Victor Comerchero's *Nathanael West: The Ironic Prophet*. Mr. Comerchero uses Eliot's poem as a way to read *The Day of the Locust*.

6. Daniel Fuchs, *Low Company*, in *3 Novels by Daniel Fuchs* (New York, 1961), pp. 28–29. All further references to the novel are cited in the text and refer to this edition.

7. Cleanth Brooks, "The Waste Land: Critique of the Myth," in Jay Martin, ed., *A Collection of Critical Essays on "The Waste Land"* (Englewood Cliffs, N.J., p. 60.

8. Fuchs did read and admire Farrell. He indicates this in a letter to G. Miller, December 4, 1973. He wrote, "I used to see something of Farrell in the old days, liked and admired his work and him personally."

9. Edgar M. Branch, *James T. Farrell* (New York, 1971), p. 52.

10. James T. Farrell, *Judgement Day* (1935; rpt. New York, 1958), p. 509.

11. Randall Reid, *The Fiction of Nathanael West* (Chicago, 1971), p. 144.

12. Ibid., p. 145.

13. Strauss, p. 6.

14. Moss, p. 41.

15. Alfred Kazin, review of *Low Company*, *New York Herald Tribune Books*, February 14, 1937. p. 8.

16. Richard H. Pells, *Radical Visions and American Dreams* (New York, 1973), p. 240.

Chapter Five

(Note: "Williamsburg in Technicolor" is Irving Howe's phrase)

1. Daniel Fuchs, "Days in the Gardens of Hollywood," *New York Times Book Review*, July 18, 1971.

2. Ibid.

3. Daniel Fuchs, "Writing for the Movies," *Commentary*, February 1962, p. 114.

4. Carolyn See, "The Hollywood Novel: The American Dream Cheat," in David Madden, ed., *Tough Guy Writers of the Thirties* (Carbondale, 1968), p. 199.

5. Edmund Wilson, "The Boys in the Back Room," in *Classics and Commercials* (1950; rpt. New York, 1962), p. 46.

6. Frederick Jackson Turner, *The Frontier in American History* (New York, 1920), pp. 2–3.

7. John Steinbeck, *The Grapes of Wrath* (New York, 1939), pp. 309–310.

8. Jonas Spatz, *Hollywood in Fiction* (The Hague, 1969), p. 16.

9. Ibid., p. 17.

10. Wilson, p. 46.

11. See, p. 200.

12. *New Yorker*, August 6, 1938.

13. "Writing for the Movies," p. 107.

14. *New Yorker*, August 1, 1953.

15. *New Yorker*, October 3, 1953.

16. *New Yorker*, July 10, 1954.

17. This probably refers to the death of Fuchs's brother George—see Chapter 1. Fuchs' father also suffered from the furrier's disease.

18. Irving Howe's phrase.

19. Irving Howe, review of *West of the Rockies*, *Harpers*, 243 (July 1971), p. 88.

20. Richard Ellman, review of *West of the Rockies*, *New York Times Book Review*, June 13, 1971, p. 7.

21. Daniel Fuchs, *West of the Rockies* (New York, 1971), pp. 165–66. All further references to the novel are cited in the text and refer to this edition.

22. Stanley Kauffman, review of *West of the Rockies*, *New Republic*, 164 (May 15, 1971), p. 29.

23. Walter Wells, *Tycoons and Locusts* (Carbondale, 1973), xi.

24. Ibid.

25. Ibid.

26. Ibid.

27. Wells, p. 13.

28. Ibid.

29. Kauffmann, p. 29.

30. John Updike, review of *West of the Rockies*, *New Yorker*, October 23, 1971.

31. "Days in the Gardens of Hollywood," p. 24.

32. "Writing for the Movies," p. 108.

33. In Joan Didion's *Play It As It Lays* (1970) the protagonist, Maria Wyeth, also an actress suffering a nervous breakdown, has recurring thoughts about her abortion and her mother's death.

34. Ben Siegel, "FUCHS, Daniel," in *Contemporary Novelists*, James Vinson, ed. (New York, 1972), p. 438.

35. Fuchs uses the same phrase to describe producer Harry Cohn in "Writing for the Movies." He confirms that the description refers to Cohn in a letter to G. Miller, September 14, 1974.

36. Confirmed by Fuchs in a letter to G. Miller, September 14, 1974.

37. "Days in the Gardens of Hollywood," p. 24.

Chapter Six

1. *Stories,* with Jean Stafford, William Maxwell, John Cheever (New York, 1956).

2. Letter from Fuchs to G. Miller, December 4, 1973.

3. *New Yorker,* September 24, 1938.

4. *New Yorker,* December 25, 1937.

5. *New Yorker,* August 20, 1938.

6. *New Yorker,* October 14, 1939.

7. *New Yorker,* May 30, 1942.

8. *New Yorker,* July 11, 1953.

9. *New Yorker,* April 8, 1939.

10. *Mademoiselle,* April 1940.

11. *New Yorker,* September 2, 1939.

12. *New Yorker,* August 10, 1940.

13. *Scribner's,* February 1938.

14. *Red Book,* April 1939.

15. *Southern Review,* Spring 1942.

16. Irving Howe, "Daniel Fuchs' Williamsburg Trilogy: A Cigarette and a Window," in *Proletarian Writers of the Thirties,* p. 101.

17. Ibid.

Selected Bibliography

PRIMARY SOURCES

1. Fiction (published in book form)
Summer in Williamsburg. New York: Vanguard Press, 1934.
Homage to Blenholt. New York: Vanguard Press, 1936.
Low Company. New York: Vanguard Press, 1937.
Stories, with Jean Stafford, William Maxwell, John Cheever. New York: Farrar, Straus and Cudahy, 1956.
3 Novels by Daniel Fuchs (includes *Summer in Williamsburg, Homage to Blenholt,* and *Low Company,* with an introduction by the author). New York: Basic Books, 1961.
West of the Rockies. New York: Alfred Knopf, 1971.

2. Stories
   A. From the *New Yorker*
      "Crap Game"—Dec. 25, 1937.
      "A Hollywood Diary"—Aug. 6, 1938.
      "The Apathetic Bookie Joint"—Aug. 20, 1938.
      "People on a Planet"—Sept. 24, 1938.
      "The Man from Mars"—April 8, 1939.
      "Love in Brooklyn"—Sept. 2, 1939.
      "The Morose Policeman"—Oct. 14, 1939.
      "There's Always Honolulu"—Aug. 10, 1940.
      "The Sun Goes Down"—Sept. 14, 1940.
      "The Language of Love"—Dec. 14, 1940.
      "Loew's Kings, the Chinks, and a Ride Home"—April 5, 1941.
      "A Clean, Quiet House"—May 30, 1942.
      "Man in the Middle of the Ocean"—July 11, 1953.
      "Ecossaise, Berceuse, Polonaise"—Aug. 1, 1953.
      "Twilight in Southern California"—Oct. 3, 1953.
      "The Golden West"—July 10, 1954.
   B. From *Collier's*
      "My Sister Who is Famous"—Sept. 4, 1937.
      "Such a Nice Spring Day"—April 23, 1938.
      "Getaway Day"—Sept. 10, 1938.
      "Lucky Loser"—Oct. 15, 1938.

"A Matter of Pride"—Oct. 22, 1938.
"Life Sentence"—Nov. 19, 1938.
"If a Man Answers, Hang Up"—April 22, 1939.
"Crazy Over Pigeons"—April 29, 1939.
"Not to the Swift"—May 13, 1939.
"Toilers of the Screen"—July 8, 1939.
"A Mink Coat Each Morning"—Jan. 27, 1940.
"Pug in an Opera Hat"—Mar. 23, 1940.
"Daring Young Man"—Aug. 24, 1940.
"Racing is a Business"—Oct. 5, 1940.
"The Fabulous Rubio"—Jan. 4, 1941.
"Strange Things Happen in Brooklyn"—Feb. 1, 1941.
C. From the *Saturday Evening Post*
"Last Fall"—Mar. 5, 1938.
"Fortune and Men's Eyes"—Dec. 10, 1938.
D. From the *New Republic*
"Where Al Capone Grew Up"—Sept. 9, 1931.
"The Politician"—Oct. 11, 1939.
E. From *Harpers Bazaar*
"Shun All Care"—May 1938.
"The Hosiery Shop"—Sept. 1, 1939.
F. From *Esquire*
"Give Hollywood a Chance" (a satire)—Dec. 1938.
"The Woman in Buffalo"—April 1939.
G. Other Short Stories
"Pioneers! O Pioneers!"—in *Story in America*, ed. Whit Burnett and
    Martha Foley (New York: The Vanguard Press, 1934).
"Dream City or the Drugged Lake"—*Cinema Arts*, Summer 1937.
"The Amazing Mystery at Storick, Dorschi, Pflaumer, Inc."—
    Scribner's, Feb. 1938.
"A Girl Like Cele"—*Red Book*, April 1939.
"The First Smell of Spring, and Brooklyn"—*Mademoiselle*, April 1940.
"Okay, Mr. Pappendas, Okay"—*Southern Review*, Spring 1942.
"Ivanov's 'The Adventures of a Fakir': A Story"—*Commentary*, June
    1975.

3. Novella
  A. *The Long Green*—*Cosmopolitan*, Feb. 1951.

4. Essays
  A. "Writing for the Movies"—*Commentary*, Feb. 1962.
  B. "Days in the Gardens of Hollywood"—*New York Times Book Review*,
     July 18, 1971.
  C. "The Silents Spoke to the Immigrants"—*New York Times*, October 17,
     1971.

5. Screenplays
(Carol Reed's film *Trapeze* was based in part on Fuchs's "That Daring Young Man." Fuchs also wrote the screenplay for *Ocean's 11* but had his name removed from the film.)

   A. *The Day the Bookies Wept*—from a story by Daniel Fuchs; screenplay by Bert Granet and George Jeske (1939).
   B. *The Big Shot*—original screenplay by Bertram Millhauser, Abem Finkel, and Daniel Fuchs (1942).
   C. *The Hard Way*—screenplay by Daniel Fuchs and Peter Viertel (1943).
   D. *Between Two Worlds*—screenplay by Daniel Fuchs; based on a play by Sutton Vane (1944).
   E. *The Gangster*—screenplay by Daniel Fuchs; based on his novel *Low Company* (1947).
   F. *Hollow Triumph* (also known as *The Scar*)—screenplay by Daniel Fuchs; based on a novel by Murray Forbes (1948).
   G. *Criss Cross*—screenplay by Daniel Fuchs; based on a novel by Don Tracy (1949).
   H. *Panic in the Streets*—based on a story by Edna and Edward Anhalt; adaptation by Daniel Fuchs; screenplay by Richard Murphy (1950).
   I. *Storm Warning*—screenplay by Daniel Fuchs and Richard Brooks (1951).
   J. *Taxi*—screenplay by Daniel Fuchs and D. M. Marshman, Jr.; based on a story by Hans Jacoby and Fred Brady (1953).
   K. *The Human Jungle*—screenplay by William Sackheim and Daniel Fuchs (1954).
   L. *Love Me or Leave Me*—screenplay by Daniel Fuchs and Isobel Lenhart; from a story by Daniel Fuchs (1955).
   M. *Interlude*—screenplay by Daniel Fuchs and Franklin Coen; adaptation by Inez Cocke; based on a screenplay by Dwight Taylor and a story by James M. Cain (1957).
   N. *Jeanne Eagels*—screenplay by Daniel Fuchs, Sonya Levin, and John Fante; from a story by Daniel Fuchs (1957).

Note: There are stories by Fuchs that I have not as yet been able to trace because no complete bibliography of published works has been attempted before this, and even Fuchs himself cannot remember exact titles and dates for all of his works. For the two stories listed below, I have only Fuchs's conjectures, not having been able to verify them.

   1. "My Father's Story"—*Brooklyn Daily Eagle*, 1930.
   2. "The Village by the Sea"—*Opinion*, 1933(?).

SECONDARY SOURCES

ALLEN, WALTER. *The Modern Novel*. New York: E. P. Dutton & Co., 1965.

Provides an intelligent look at the themes of Fuchs's 1930s writing and groups Fuchs with West and Roth as writers who went beyond the economic themes of most 1930s fiction.

ANGOFF, CHARLES. Introduction to Daniel Fuchs. *The Rise of American Jewish Literature.* Ed. Charles Angoff and Meyer Levin. New York: Simon and Schuster, 1970. A brief introduction that precedes an excerpt from *Summer in Williamsburg* in an anthology of American-Jewish fiction.

BELLMAN, SAMUEL I. "Sleep, Pride, and Fantasy: Birth Traumas and Socio-Biologic Adaptation in the American-Jewish Novel." *Costerus,* 8 (1973), pp. 1–12. An article that deals with a number of American-Jewish novels, including *Homage to Blenholt,* and their preoccupation with the immigrant's physical and psychological desire to transcend his position.

BESSIE, ALVAH. *Inquisition in Eden.* New York: The Macmillan Co., 1965. An autobiographical narrative of Bessie's days in Hollywood, touching on his relationship with Fuchs.

BLOTNER, JOSEPH. *Faulkner: A Biography.* New York: Random House, 1974. Mentions Fuchs, who worked with Faulkner on the film *Background to Danger.*

CORLISS, RICHARD, ed. *The Hollywood Screenwriters.* New York: Avon Books, 1972. Contains a bibliography of Fuchs's screenwork.

FIEDLER, LESLIE. *Love and Death in the American Novel.* 1960; rev. ed. New York: Dell Publishing Co., 1966. Mentions Fuchs parenthetically as a writer who created myths of urban alienation.

———. *No! in Thunder.* New York: Stein and Day, 1972. Mentions Fuchs in an article on Malamud.

———. *To the Gentiles.* New York: Stein and Day, 1972. Discusses Fuchs's characters as *schlemiel*-victims.

———. *Unfinished Business.* New York: Stein and Day, 1972. Three of the essays reprinted in this volume mention Fuchs, as a neglected writer of the 1930s and in essays on John Peale Bishop and Henry Roth.

———. *Waiting for the End.* 1964; rpt. New York: Stein and Day, 1970. Again mentions Fuchs as a neglected 1930s writer and makes some excellent comments on his treatment of gangsters and his attitude toward Hollywood.

GROSS, THEODORE L., ed. *The Literature of American Jews.* New York: The Free Press, 1973. Contains a very brief summation of Fuchs's career.

GUTTMANN, ALLEN. *The Jewish Writer in America: Assimilation and the Crisis of Identity.* New York: Oxford University Press, 1971. A brief discussion of 1930s novels, emphasizing their comic qualities.

HOWE, IRVING. "Daniel Fuchs: Escape from Williamsburg." *Commentary,* 6 (July 1948), pp. 29–34. The best and only serious discussion of Fuchs's work.

———. "Daniel Fuchs' Williamsburg Trilogy: A Cigarette and a Window." *Proletarian Writers of the Thirties.* Ed. David Madden. Carbondale:

Southern Illinois Univ. Press, 1968. A shorter version, in which some of Howe's earlier arguments are modified.

―――. *World of Our Fathers*. New York: Harcourt, Brace, Jovanovich, 1976. Incorporates ideas from the earlier pieces.

MADDEN, DAVID, ed. *Proletarian Writers of the Thirties*. Carbondale: Southern Illinois Univ. Press, 1968. Introduction to a collection of essays on thirties writers, in which Fuchs is seen as a writer who forged a private vision.

MILLER, GABRIEL. "Screenwriter Daniel Fuchs: A Creed Grows in Brooklyn." *Los Angeles Times Book Review*, 17 April 1977, p. 3. A brief discussion of Fuchs's novels, career, and attitudes toward the film industry.

MOSS, HOWARD. *Writing Against Time*. New York: William Morrow & Co., 1969. Reprint of Moss's review of *3 Novels by Daniel Fuchs*, in which he makes some good observations, especially about Fuchs's use of comedy.

PELLS, RICHARD H. *Radical Visions and American Dreams*. New York: Harper & Row, 1973. The first study of the 1930s to come to grips with Fuchs's work, placing him in the "conservative tradition."

SHAW, IRWIN. "Daniel Fuchs' *Homage to Blenholt*." *Rediscoveries*. Ed. David Madden. New York: Crown Publishers, 1971. A complimentary essay by a friend, who touches on comedy in the novel, but provides little in the way of significant discussion.

SIEGEL, BEN. "Fuchs, Daniel." *Contemporary Novelists*. Ed. James Vinson. New York: St. Martins Press, 1972. A very intelligent evaluation of Fuchs's four novels.

SWADOS, HARVEY, ed. *The American Writer and the Great Depression*. New York: Bobbs-Merrill Co., 1966. Mentions Fuchs in highly complimentary terms in an introduction to an anthology of 1930s writing, and takes Alfred Kazin to task for leaving Fuchs out of *On Native Grounds*.

UPDIKE, JOHN. Afterword. *West of the Rockies*. 1971; rpt. New York: Popular Library, 1972. An appreciative essay (originally published in the *New Yorker*) on Fuchs's style, and *West of the Rockies* in particular.

WALDEN, DANIEL, ed. *On Being Jewish*. Greenwich, Conn.: Fawcett Publications, 1974. Mentions Fuchs mistakenly in the introduction as a social writer, though his work does not appear in the anthology.

Index